Pomegranates & Prickly Pears

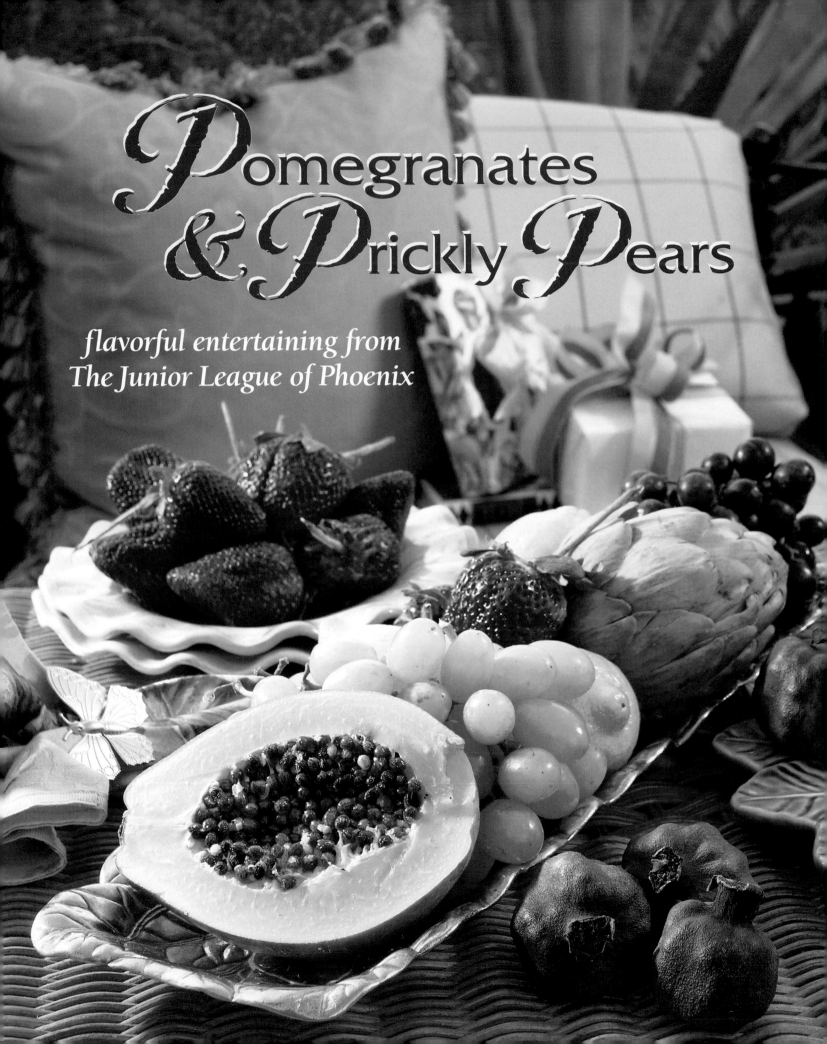

Pomegranates & Prickly Pears

flavorful entertaining from
The Junior League of Phoenix

Front cover photography © Patrick Darby
Photography credits on pages 9, 11, 37, 61, 85, 107,
131, 155, 175, 195, and 217 are an extension of
this page.

The cookbook is a collection of favorite recipes,
which are not necessarily original recipes.

Library of Congress Catalog Number: 2004110746
ISBN: 0-9613174-3-4

Edited, Designed, and Manufactured by
Favorite Recipes® Press
An imprint of

FRP

P. O. Box 305142
Nashville, Tennessee 37230
800-358-0560

Art Director: Steve Newman
Book Design: Annette Kracht
Project Editor: Debbie Van Mol
Food Photography: © R&R Images

Manufactured in the United States of America
First Printing: 2005   20,000 copies

Foreword

As a young bride, I loved to cook and try new dishes by inviting our friends for dinner. As I worked my way through many, many cookbooks, I soon realized that the Junior Leagues' were the best. They always had delicious, doable recipes that were perfect for entertaining. As I traveled about the country, my mission became seeking out the Junior League cookbook from each city I visited. I knew the dishes would work because they were used by busy, accomplished women who loved to host memorable parties but didn't want to slave in the kitchen all day.

The Junior League of Phoenix has published several marvelous cookbooks, and *Pomegranates & Prickly Pears* will be a spectacular addition to that collection. It contains mouthwatering recipes and imaginative, delightful entertaining ideas for every occasion, including children's parties and events that celebrate our outdoor lifestyle. It's a fabulous resource for year-round parties, and what a terrific gift to give to others who enjoy sharing their love through cooking! I know it's going to have a prominent spot in my culinary library.

Wishing you happy food memories,

Barbara Pool Fenzl

Barbara Pool Fenzl, CCP
Owner, Les Gourmettes Cooking School
Author of *Southwest the Beautiful Cookbook* and *Savor the Southwest*

Preface

*T*hank you for supporting the community programs of The Junior League of Phoenix by purchasing this cookbook. Not only will you enjoy the regional flavors from the Valley of the Sun, but you will also be benefiting programs that center on strengthening families.

The Junior League of Phoenix's unwavering commitment to our community is seen in so many different arenas. Founded in 1935, The Junior League of Phoenix has been instrumental in making a positive, permanent difference in the lives of thousands of families. We have been able to address many needs in the community over the past sixty-nine years, both as visionaries and problem-solvers.

Visionary in seeing unmet needs and putting volunteer hours and money into creating solutions, The Junior League of Phoenix started what is now the Ronald McDonald House, the Court Appointed Special Advocate (CASA) program, and Crisis Nursery, just to name a few. The Junior League also brought the Komen Phoenix Race for the Cure® to the Valley due to the diligence of three Junior League members who lost a friend to breast cancer. The innovative thinking of Junior League members has helped to create bridges between families in need and services that have become true necessities in our community.

The Junior League of Phoenix's membership is committed to problem-solving and helping other nonprofit organizations meet their goals and commitments. Cultural venues such as the Arizona Science Center, Phoenix Museum of History, and Orpheum Theatre have all benefited from the commitment and training of Junior League members. Through collaborative efforts, programs like Safe Return, which registers Alzheimer's patients, and Life Books, which creates scrapbooks for foster children, were able to not just survive, but thrive with the support of The Junior League of Phoenix.

Currently, The Junior League of Phoenix's community programs include Phoenix Family Museum, which plans to offer families a fun, informative place to interact and learn upon opening; Read to Me Book Parties, which support home-based and low-income child care centers with books and literacy materials; The World is Mine, in which Junior League members, through a partnership with the Boys & Girls Club of the East Valley, help to mentor at-risk, preteen girls; and Women Living Free, which partners Junior League members with women coming out of prison, helping them to get acclimated back into the community.

Junior League of Phoenix members volunteer more than 100,000 hours per year and have given more than $3,000,000 back into the community. We raise money for our community programs through annual fund-raisers, as well as through sales of our wonderful cookbooks. We are very grateful for your help in promoting our vision that strong families are the foundation of a viable community. By purchasing *Pomegranates & Prickly Pears*, you are helping us further serve the community through strengthening the family.

We wish you many memorable meals,
The Junior League of Phoenix, Inc.

Acknowledgments & Sponsors

The Junior League of Phoenix graciously acknowledges the generosity of the following contributors:

Gold Place Setting

3rios fototeca—Scenic Photography
AJ's Fine Foods—Food Photography
Desert Botanical Gardens—Cover Location and Scenic Photography
R&R Images—Cover and Food Photography, Chef Photo

Silver Place Setting

Arizona Culinary Institute
Linthicum Custom Builders
Pembrook Lane Interiors—Cover Photography Stylist
Sportsman's Fine Wines and Spirits—Chef Wine Pairings
West Coast Turf

Completer Set

Fiesta Bowl—Scenic Photography
Mary Dell Pritzlaff

Celebrated Chefs

The Arizona Kitchen at the Wigwam Resort & Golf Club, John Conrad II
Roaring Fork, Robert McGrath
Arcadia Farms, Jeff Blake
Barrio Café, Silvana Salcido Esparza
Bistro 24 at The Ritz-Carlton, Robert Graham
Cowboy Ciao, Bernie Kantak
Durant's, Kenneth Giordano
Eddie V's Edgewater Grill, James Robert
elements, Charles Wiley
Franco's Italian Caffé, Franco Fazzuoli
Les Gourmettes Cooking School, Barbara Pool Fenzl
LON's at the hermosa, Fernando Divina
Mancuso's, Gabriel Baza
Zinc Bistro, Matthew Carter

Cookbook Development Committee

Chair
Erica Aeed TeKampe

Design
Annette Kracht

Recipes
Marci Symington

Non-Recipe Text
Julie Foster

Marketing
Kristy Kevitt
Pamela Bachmann
Karen Eiserloh

Fund-raising Council Director
Kiffie Robbins

Mission

The Junior League of Phoenix, Incorporated, is an organization of women committed to promoting voluntarism, developing the potential of women, and improving the community through the effective action and leadership of trained volunteers. Its purpose is exclusively educational and charitable.

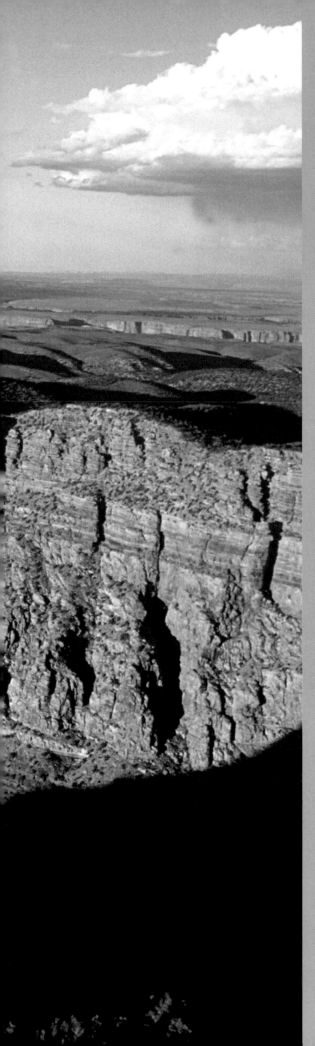

Pomegranates
& Prickly Pears

photo donated by 3rios fototeca
photo © Adalberto R. Lanz

When some people think of The Junior League, they think of women in white gloves enjoying a lovely lunch. However, Junior League of Phoenix members spend more than 100,000 hours per year on hands-on projects benefiting the community. Over the years, members have helped develop a garden for disabled children, provided after-school support to homeless children in a shelter, and mentored women being released from prison. These are just a few of the many ways that The Junior League of Phoenix has put its hands on the community. And after all the hard work, members do enjoy time to gather and gab with friends, especially when it happens over lunch.

Ladies Who Lunch

photo donated by The Desert Botanical Gardens
photo © Jennifer Johnston

Beverages
Citrus Punch
Bridesmaid
Minted Vodka Lemonade

Appetizers
Herbed Cream Cheese Cucumber Rounds
Smoked Salmon Tartare on Toast Points
Amaretto Fruit Dip
Panko-Crusted Crab Cake Bites with
       Dijon Rémoulade
Tomato, Basil and Mozzarella Tart

Egg Dishes
Eggs Benedict with Blender Hollandaise Sauce
Five-Layer Quiche
Green Chile and Chorizo Breakfast Strata

Salads and Sides
Asparagus Salad with Walnut Oil Vinaigrette
French Potato Salad
Classic Cobb Salad
Curried Chicken and Peach Salad
Ahi Tuna Niçoise Salad
Shrimp Salad
Gorgonzola Soufflé

Breads
Cherry Streusel Coffee Cake
Chocolate Hazelnut Biscotti
Berry Crème Fraîche Scones with Lemon Glaze
Amaretto French Toast
Sour Cream Cinnamon Twists
Sticky Buns

Desserts
Lemon Crème Brûlée
Chocolate Coffee Bean Cheesecake
Cream Cheese Pound Cake
Tartes aux Pommes with Caramel

Ladies Who Lunch

lunches and brunches

Citrus Punch

Serves 20

1 (46-ounce) can each pineapple juice and apple juice
1 (12-ounce) can frozen lemonade concentrate, thawed
1/4 cup sugar
4 (1-liter) bottles ginger ale, chilled

*C*ombine the pineapple juice, apple juice, lemonade concentrate and sugar in a large pitcher and stir until the sugar dissolves. Pour the juice mixture evenly into 4 resealable plastic freezer bags and seal tightly. Freeze until firm.

Thaw the desired amount of frozen juice mixture in a punch bowl until slushy, adding 1 liter of ginger ale per bag, and stir gently. Ladle into punch cups.

For variety, float a **Citrus Ice Ring** in the punch. Create the ice ring by placing the desired amount and kinds of sliced fresh fruit in a circular mold and cover generously with water. Freeze until firm and invert into the punch bowl.

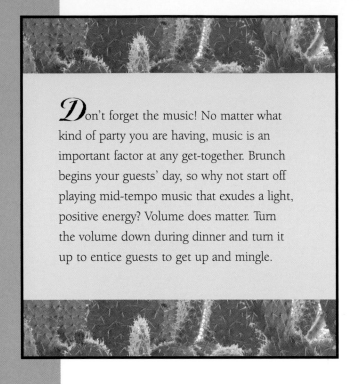

*D*on't forget the music! No matter what kind of party you are having, music is an important factor at any get-together. Brunch begins your guests' day, so why not start off playing mid-tempo music that exudes a light, positive energy? Volume does matter. Turn the volume down during dinner and turn it up to entice guests to get up and mingle.

Bridesmaid

Serves 1

1 lime wedge
Pink-tinted or white sugar to taste, or a mixture of the two
2 tablespoons (about) raspberry sorbet
2 ounces ginger ale
4 ounces sparkling wine

*R*ub the rim of a chilled margarita or Champagne glass with the lime wedge. Dip the rim into sugar and rotate gently to cover evenly. Add the sorbet to the sugar-rimmed glass and pour the ginger ale down the side of the glass to prevent foam from forming as it hits the sorbet. Add the sparkling wine in the same manner and serve immediately.

Minted Vodka Lemonade

Serves 6

1 cup packed fresh mint leaves, chopped
2/3 cup sugar
1 1/2 cups vodka

1 cup fresh lemon juice
Crushed ice
Sprigs of fresh mint

*C*ombine the chopped mint and sugar in a large bowl. Stir in the vodka and lemon juice. Chill, covered, for 30 minutes or for up to 2 hours. Strain the mint mixture into a pitcher, discarding the solids.

Fill six 6- to 8-ounce glasses with crushed ice and pour the lemonade evenly into the glasses. Garnish with sprigs of fresh mint.

Herbed Cream Cheese Cucumber Rounds

Makes 32 rounds

4 ounces cream cheese or chèvre, softened
2 tablespoons thinly sliced fresh mint
2 teaspoons finely chopped fresh chives
1/2 teaspoon finely grated lemon zest
1/4 teaspoon fresh lemon juice
1/8 teaspoon salt

1/16 teaspoon cayenne pepper, or to taste
1/2 seedless cucumber
3 radishes
Coarse salt to taste
Small fresh mint leaves
Finely grated lemon zest to taste

*C*ombine the cream cheese, 2 tablespoons mint, chives, 1/2 teaspoon lemon zest, lemon juice, 1/8 teaspoon salt and cayenne pepper in a bowl and mix well.

Cut the cucumber into thirty-two 1/8-inch rounds. Trim the bottoms of the radishes and slice into thirty-two 1/16-inch rounds. Top each cucumber slice with a radish slice and 1/2 teaspoon of the cream cheese mixture. Sprinkle with coarse salt and arrange on a serving platter. Garnish with mint leaves and finely grated lemon zest to taste. Serve immediately. Serve on melba toast rounds if desired. Or, spoon the cream cheese mixture into a pastry bag fitted with a rosette tip and pipe rosettes onto the cucumber rounds.

Smoked Salmon Tartare on Toast Points

Serves 6

6 slices bread, crusts removed
3/4 cup chopped smoked salmon
2 tablespoons minced red onion
2 tablespoons drained capers
2 tablespoons olive oil
1 tablespoon lemon juice
Freshly ground pepper to taste
6 tablespoons sour cream
1 tablespoon chopped fresh dill weed
Sprigs of fresh dill weed
Lemon wedges

*I*f you would like to try your hand at preparing your own **Gravlax**, try this simple recipe. Combine 1 cup kosher salt, 1/2 cup chopped fresh dill weed, 1/4 cup sugar, 3 tablespoons vodka, 2 tablespoons grated orange zest and freshly ground pepper to taste in a bowl and mix well. Arrange one 4-pound salmon fillet skin side down on several large sheets of plastic wrap. Cover the entire surface of the salmon with the salt mixture and wrap tightly in the plastic wrap. Arrange the salmon skin side down on a sheet pan and weight down with a heavy skillet or brick wrapped in plastic wrap. Chill for 24 hours. Remove the salmon from the refrigerator and wipe off the salt mixture. Rinse under cold water and pat dry.

*P*reheat the oven to 375 degrees. Cut each bread slice into 4 triangles and arrange the triangles in a single layer on a baking sheet. Toast until brown on both sides.

Combine the salmon, onion, capers, olive oil and lemon juice in a bowl and mix well. Season with pepper. Mix the sour cream and chopped dill weed in a bowl. Top each toast point with about 1 1/2 teaspoons of the tartare and a small dollop of the sour cream mixture. Sprinkle with pepper. Arrange on a small platter garnished with sprigs of fresh dill weed and lemon wedges.

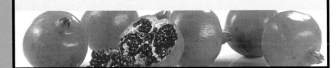

Amaretto Fruit Dip

Makes 2 1/2 cups

2 cups sour cream
1/4 cup packed brown sugar
2 to 4 tablespoons amaretto

*C*ombine the sour cream, brown sugar and liqueur in a bowl and mix well. Chill, covered, for 8 to 10 hours. Serve with chunks of fresh fruit.

Panko-Crusted Crab Cake Bites with Dijon Rémoulade

Makes 2 dozen crab cakes

1/4 cup chopped celery
1/4 cup minced fresh chives
1/4 cup mayonnaise
1 egg, lightly beaten
2 teaspoons Dijon mustard
1 teaspoon fresh lime juice
1/4 teaspoon Tabasco sauce
12 ounces cooked crab meat
1 1/4 cups panko
Salt and pepper to taste
Fresh chives
Dijon Rémoulade (sidebar)

*P*reheat the oven to 475 degrees. Combine the celery, 1/4 cup chives, mayonnaise, egg, mustard, lime juice and Tabasco sauce in a bowl and mix well with a fork. Fold in the crab meat and 1/4 cup of the bread crumbs. Season with salt and pepper.

Shape the crab meat mixture into 24 cakes, approximately 1/2 inch thick and 2 inches in diameter. Coat the crab cakes with the remaining 1 cup bread crumbs. Arrange the crab cakes in a single layer on an oiled baking sheet.

Bake for 15 to 18 minutes or until brown. Garnish with fresh chives and serve immediately with Dijon Rémoulade. You may substitute chopped cooked shrimp for the crab meat.

*S*erve this quick and easy **Dijon Rémoulade** with Panko-Crusted Crab Cake Bites or with your favorite seafood recipe. Combine 1 cup mayonnaise, 2 tablespoons finely chopped green onions, 2 tablespoons minced fresh parsley, 1 tablespoon chopped capers, 2 to 3 tablespoons fresh lemon juice, 1 teaspoon Worcestershire sauce, 2 teaspoons whole grain Dijon mustard, salt to taste, black pepper to taste and cayenne pepper to taste in a bowl and mix well. You may prepare in advance and store, covered, in the refrigerator for several days.

Tomato, Basil and Mozzarella Tart

Serves 6 to 8

1 (17-ounce) package frozen puff pastry,
    thawed using package directions
1 egg, beaten
1 cup (4 ounces) finely grated
    Parmesan cheese
1 pound Roma tomatoes, cut crosswise into
    1/4-inch slices
1/2 teaspoon salt

2 garlic cloves, minced or crushed
2 tablespoons extra-virgin olive oil
1/16 teaspoon salt
Ground pepper to taste
8 ounces low-moisture whole milk mozzarella
    cheese, shredded
2 tablespoons coarsely chopped fresh basil

*A*djust the oven rack to the lower-middle position of the oven and preheat to 425 degrees. Unfold the pastry sheets on a lightly floured work surface. To form the tart shell, brush some of the egg along the edge of 1 sheet of the pastry. Overlap the second sheet of pastry by 1 inch and press together to seal. Smooth out the seam using a rolling pin. The pastry rectangle should measure approximately 9×18 inches. Trim the edges straight with a pizza wheel or sharp knife.

Cut one 1-inch strip from the long side of the pastry. Cut another 1-inch strip from the same side. Cut one 1-inch strip from the short side of the pastry. Cut another 1-inch strip from the same side. Transfer the pastry rectangle and strips of pastry to a baking sheet lined with baking parchment. Brush the strips with some of the egg. Gently press the long strips of pastry onto the long edge of the shell and brush with some of the egg. Repeat the process with the short strips of pastry. Trim the excess dough from the corners. Sprinkle the Parmesan cheese over the shell and pierce with a fork. Bake for 13 to 15 minutes; reduce the oven temperature to 350 degrees. Bake for 13 to 15 minutes longer or until light brown. Let stand until cool. Maintain the oven temperature.

Arrange the tomato slices in a single layer on paper towels and sprinkle with 1/2 teaspoon salt. Let stand for 30 minutes and pat dry. Mix the garlic, olive oil, 1/16 teaspoon salt and pepper in a bowl.

Sprinkle the mozzarella cheese over the warm tart shell. Shingle the tomato slices widthwise on top of the cheese, about 4 slices per row, and brush with the garlic mixture. Bake for 15 to 17 minutes or until the shell is deep golden brown and the cheese melts. Cool for 5 minutes and sprinkle with the basil. Remove to a cutting board or serving platter and cut into wedges. Add prosciutto or substitute smoked mozzarella for the whole milk mozzarella if desired. You may bake the tart shell up to 2 days in advance and store, wrapped in plastic wrap, at room temperature.

Eggs Benedict with Blender Hollandaise Sauce

Serves 8

Hollandaise Sauce

3 egg yolks
1 tablespoon water
1/8 teaspoon salt
1/8 teaspoon white pepper
1/8 teaspoon cayenne pepper
1/8 teaspoon hot sauce (optional)
1/2 cup (1 stick) butter
1 tablespoon lemon juice
1 to 2 tablespoons hot tap water (optional)

Eggs Benedict

8 slices Canadian bacon
8 eggs
4 English muffins, split and toasted

*F*or the sauce, combine the egg yolks, water, salt, white pepper, cayenne pepper and hot sauce in a blender and process until blended. Heat the butter and lemon juice in a saucepan until almost boiling, stirring occasionally.

Add the hot butter mixture to the egg mixture gradually, processing constantly at high speed for 30 seconds or until thickened. Immediately add the hot water and process until smooth if the sauce becomes too thick or curdles. If you are concerned about using raw egg yolks, use eggs pasteurized in their shells, which are sold at some specialty food stores, or use an equivalent amount of pasteurized egg substitute.

For the eggs, sauté the bacon in a skillet until brown. Poach the eggs for approximately 2 1/2 minutes or fry if desired. To serve, top each muffin half with 1 slice of bacon and 1 poached egg. Drizzle with the sauce and serve immediately.

Five-Layer Quiche

Serves 6 to 8

4 (4-ounce) cans whole green chiles, drained
1 pound bacon, crisp-cooked and crumbled
1 small onion, chopped

1 pound Monterey Jack cheese, shredded
1 pound sharp Cheddar cheese, shredded
12 eggs

*P*reheat the oven to 350 degrees. Slit the green chiles lengthwise to but not through the other side and lay flat over the bottom of a 9×13-inch baking pan. Sprinkle with the bacon, onion, Monterey Jack cheese and Cheddar cheese in the order listed. Whisk the eggs in a bowl until blended and pour over the prepared layers. Bake for 45 minutes or until a wooden pick inserted in the center comes out clean. For variety, add some of your favorite ingredients prior to the cheese layer.

Green Chile and Chorizo Breakfast Strata

Serves 6

2 pounds chorizo or soyrizo, casings removed
   and sliced
1/2 cup chopped yellow onion
1 garlic clove, minced
2 1/2 cups milk
5 eggs
1 teaspoon cumin
1/2 teaspoon salt

1/4 teaspoon pepper
6 (4 1/2×6 1/2-inch) slices sourdough bread,
   crusts removed
1 3/4 cups (7 ounces) shredded hot
   Pepper Jack cheese
3 poblano chiles, roasted, seeded,
   peeled and chopped
1/2 cup chopped fresh cilantro

*P*reheat the oven to 350 degrees. Sauté the sausage, onion and garlic in a large heavy skillet over medium-low heat for 15 minutes or until the sausage is cooked through. Remove the sausage mixture with a slotted spoon to a plate lined with paper towels to drain.

Whisk the milk, eggs, cumin, salt and pepper in a bowl until blended. Arrange 2 slices of the bread in a buttered 8-cup soufflé dish or baking dish. Layer with 3/4 cup of the cheese, 1/2 of the poblano chiles, 1/2 of the cilantro and 1/2 of the sausage mixture. Pour 1/3 of the egg mixture over the prepared layers.

Repeat the layering process with 2 more bread slices, 3/4 cup of the cheese, the remaining poblano chiles, remaining cilantro and remaining sausage mixture. Pour 1/2 of the remaining egg mixture over the top. Layer with the remaining 2 bread slices and remaining egg mixture and sprinkle with the remaining 1/4 cup cheese. Bake for 55 minutes or until brown and puffed. Let stand for 5 minutes before serving.

Asparagus Salad with Walnut Oil Vinaigrette

Serves 6 to 8

Walnut Oil Vinaigrette
1/4 cup white wine vinegar
1 tablespoon minced shallot
2 teaspoons Dijon mustard
3/4 teaspoon salt
1/2 teaspoon freshly ground pepper
1/2 cup vegetable oil
1/4 cup walnut oil

Salad
2 pounds asparagus, trimmed and steamed
   until al dente
1/3 cup chopped walnuts, toasted
1 tablespoon chopped fresh parsley
Parmigiano-Reggiano shavings to taste
Salt and freshly ground pepper to taste

For the vinaigrette, whisk the vinegar, shallot, mustard, salt and pepper in a bowl until mixed. Add the vegetable oil gradually, whisking constantly. Whisk in the walnut oil until incorporated.

For the salad, arrange the asparagus on a platter and drizzle with the vinaigrette. Sprinkle with the walnuts, parsley and cheese. Taste and season with salt and pepper if desired.

French Potato Salad

Serves 6 to 8

1 pound small white potatoes
1 pound small red potatoes
Salt to taste
2 tablespoons dry white wine
2 tablespoons chicken stock or broth
3 tablespoons Champagne vinegar
1 teaspoon Dijon mustard
1/2 teaspoon kosher salt

1/4 teaspoon freshly ground pepper
1/2 cup plus 2 tablespoons olive oil
1/4 cup minced whole scallions
2 tablespoons minced fresh dill weed
2 tablespoons minced fresh flat-leaf parsley
2 tablespoons julienned fresh basil
1 1/2 teaspoons kosher salt
1/2 teaspoon pepper

Boil the potatoes in boiling salted water in a saucepan for 20 to 30 minutes or just until cooked through and drain in a colander. Drape the potatoes with a tea towel and allow to steam for 10 minutes. Cut into quarters and place in a bowl. Add the wine and stock to the warm potatoes and toss gently to coat. Let stand until the potatoes soak up the liquids. Whisk the vinegar, mustard, 1/2 teaspoon salt and 1/4 teaspoon pepper in a bowl. Whisk in the olive oil gradually until incorporated. Add the vinaigrette to the potatoes and toss gently. Stir in the scallions, dill weed, parsley, basil, 1 1/2 teaspoons salt and 1/2 teaspoon pepper. Serve warm, at room temperature or chilled.

Classic Cobb Salad

Serves 4 to 6

Dijon Vinaigrette

1/2 cup extra-virgin olive oil
Juice of 1 lemon
1 garlic clove, crushed
2 tablespoons red wine vinegar
1 teaspoon Dijon mustard
1 teaspoon Worcestershire sauce
1/2 teaspoon salt
1/4 teaspoon sugar
1/8 teaspoon pepper

Salad

3 boneless skinless chicken breasts
Salt and pepper to taste
1 large head romaine, torn
1 bunch watercress, stemmed
1 pint grape tomatoes, cut into halves
3 eggs, hard-cooked and coarsely chopped
2 avocados, coarsely chopped
8 slices bacon, crisp-cooked and crumbled
1/2 cup (2 ounces) crumbled blue cheese
3 tablespoons minced fresh chives

*F*or the vinaigrette, combine the olive oil, lemon juice, garlic, vinegar, mustard, Worcestershire sauce, salt, sugar and pepper in a jar with a tight-fitting lid and seal tightly. Shake to mix. You may prepare up to 1 day in advance and store, covered, in the refrigerator. Bring to room temperature before serving.

For the salad, arrange the oven rack 6 inches from the heat source and preheat the broiler. Sprinkle the chicken with salt and pepper and arrange on a broiler pan sprayed with nonstick cooking spray. Broil for 4 to 8 minutes or until light brown and turn. Broil for 6 to 8 minutes longer or until cooked through. Chop the chicken into bite-size pieces.

To serve, toss the romaine, watercress and 5 tablespoons of the vinaigrette in a bowl until coated and arrange on a large serving platter. Toss the chicken with 1/4 cup of the vinaigrette in the same bowl and arrange along 1 edge of the platter. Toss the tomatoes with 1 tablespoon of the vinaigrette in the same bowl and arrange along the opposite edge of the platter. Place the chopped eggs and chopped avocados in separate rows near the center of the platter and drizzle with the remaining vinaigrette. Sprinkle with the bacon, cheese and chives and serve immediately.

Curried Chicken and Peach Salad

Serves 4

Creamy Curry Dressing

6 tablespoons mayonnaise

6 tablespoons sour cream

3/4 teaspoon lemon juice

1/2 teaspoon curry powder, or to taste

1/8 teaspoon salt

1/8 teaspoon ginger

1/8 teaspoon cinnamon

Salad

8 cups torn Bibb lettuce

2 cups chopped cooked chicken

2 cups sliced peeled fresh peaches (about 1 1/4 pounds)

1/2 cup raisins

Bibb lettuce leaves

2 tablespoons chopped fresh chives

*F*or the dressing, combine the mayonnaise, sour cream, lemon juice, curry powder, salt, ginger and cinnamon in a bowl and mix well.

For the salad, toss the torn lettuce, chicken, peaches, raisins and desired amount of dressing in a bowl until coated. Spoon 2 cups of the salad onto each of 4 lettuce-lined plates and sprinkle with the chives. Serve immediately.

Ahi Tuna Niçoise Salad

Serves 4

Niçoise Vinaigrette

1/4 cup fresh lemon juice
1/4 cup red wine vinegar
1/4 cup Dijon mustard
2 tablespoons minced garlic
2 tablespoons minced shallots
1 1/2 cups extra-virgin olive oil
Kosher salt and freshly ground pepper to taste

Salad

4 ounces haricots verts or green beans, trimmed
Kosher salt and freshly ground pepper to taste
1 onion, cut into 1/4-inch slices
2 tablespoons extra-virgin olive oil
1 red bell pepper, roasted, peeled, seeded and
    cut into 1/4-inch strips

1 yellow bell pepper, roasted, peeled, seeded
    and cut into 1/4-inch strips
2 (6-ounce) center-cut Ahi tuna fillets
Cracked coriander seeds to taste
Cracked pepper to taste
2 to 2 1/2 tablespoons olive oil
4 cups mixed baby lettuce
1 cup red and yellow pear tomatoes or cherry
    tomatoes, cut into halves
6 ounces fingerling or new potatoes, boiled
    and cut into quarters
6 tablespoons pitted niçoise olives
2 eggs, hard-cooked and cut into halves
1/4 cup chopped fresh chives

*F*or the vinaigrette, whisk the lemon juice, vinegar, mustard, garlic and shallots in a bowl. Add the olive oil gradually, whisking constantly until incorporated. Season with salt and pepper. Store, covered, in the refrigerator, whisking before serving.

For the salad, blanch the haricots verts in boiling water in a saucepan. Immediately plunge into a bowl of ice water to stop the cooking process. Drain and season with salt and pepper. Sauté the onion in 2 tablespoons olive oil in a sauté pan for 10 minutes or until caramelized, stirring constantly. Season with salt and pepper and remove to a bowl. Toss the roasted bell peppers in a bowl. Sprinkle the tuna with coriander seeds and cracked pepper. Sear the fillets in 2 to 2 1/2 tablespoons olive oil in a small saucepan over high heat for 1 to 2 minutes or until brown on both sides, keeping the centers rare. Remove to a hard surface and slice the fillets.

To serve, toss the haricots verts, onion, roasted bell peppers, lettuce, tomatoes, potatoes and olives with 3/4 cup of the vinaigrette in a bowl and arrange on a serving platter. Layer with the sliced tuna, top with eggs and sprinkle with the chives. Or, toss the lettuce with 3/4 cup of the vinaigrette in a large bowl and arrange on a serving platter. Mound 3 portions each of the haricots verts, onion, roasted bell peppers, tomatoes, potatoes and olives on a platter. Arrange the haricots verts in a clockwise fashion at 1, 5 and 9 o'clock over the lettuce. Place the remaining ingredients in between the haricots verts. Arrange the tuna slices and egg slices in the center and sprinkle with the chives.

Shrimp Salad

Serves 4 as an entrée, or 8 as an appetizer

2 (11-ounce) cans mandarin oranges
1 1/2 pounds medium shrimp, peeled and deveined
Salt to taste
2 tablespoons olive oil
1 teaspoon minced garlic
1/2 cup mayonnaise
3 tablespoons ketchup
1 1/2 tablespoons Cognac
2 teaspoons fresh lime juice
1 teaspoon curry powder
1/2 teaspoon sugar
1/2 teaspoon cayenne pepper
1/4 teaspoon Tabasco sauce, or to taste
4 large avocados, cut into halves
4 canned hearts of palm, rinsed and cut into 1/2-inch pieces
Butter lettuce leaves
Grape clusters
1 tablespoon chopped fresh dill weed

*T*o freeze fresh shrimp, place the shrimp in a freezer container and cover completely with ice water. When thawed under cold running water and then cooked, the shrimp will taste just like fresh.

*D*rain the oranges, reserving 1 tablespoon of the juice. Chill the oranges in a bowl in the refrigerator. Poach the shrimp in boiling salted water in a saucepan for 1 to 2 minutes; drain. Toss the warm shrimp with the reserved juice, olive oil and garlic in a bowl. Cool to room temperature. Chill, covered, for 8 to 10 hours. Combine the mayonnaise, ketchup, brandy, lime juice, curry powder, sugar, cayenne pepper and Tabasco sauce in a bowl and mix well. Chill, covered, for 8 to 10 hours.

Drain the chilled oranges. Cut the avocado halves lengthwise into quarters and cut the quarters into 1/2-inch pieces. Fold the oranges, avocados and hearts of palm into the shrimp mixture. Spoon the shrimp mixture evenly onto 4 butter lettuce-lined salad plates. Garnish with grape clusters and spoon some of the mayonnaise mixture over each salad. Sprinkle with the dill weed.

Gorgonzola Soufflé

Serves 4

4 tablespoons ($^1/_2$ stick) unsalted butter, softened
4 teaspoons grated Parmesan cheese
4 teaspoons dry bread crumbs
3 tablespoons flour
$^3/_4$ cup milk
$3^1/_2$ ounces Gorgonzola cheese, shredded
2 egg yolks
3 egg whites
$^1/_4$ teaspoon hot sauce
$^1/_8$ teaspoon freshly grated or ground nutmeg
Salt and pepper to taste

$\mathcal{P}$reheat the oven to 400 degrees. Generously butter four 4-ounce ramekins with 1 tablespoon of the butter. Mix the Parmesan cheese and bread crumbs in a bowl and sprinkle the crumb mixture over the bottoms and sides of the prepared ramekins.

Heat the remaining 3 tablespoons butter in a large saucepan over low heat. Whisk in the flour until blended. Cook for 3 to 5 minutes or until a nutty aroma develops, whisking constantly. Add the milk gradually, whisking constantly. Cook for 3 to 4 minutes longer or until thickened and of a sauce consistency, whisking constantly. Remove from the heat and pour into a large bowl. Add the Gorgonzola cheese and stir until blended.

Whisk the egg yolks in a bowl until blended. Add $^1/_4$ cup of the cheese sauce to the egg yolks, whisking constantly. Whisk the egg yolk mixture into the remaining cheese sauce. Whisk the egg whites in a bowl until soft peaks form and stir $^1/_4$ of the egg whites into the egg yolk mixture. Fold in the remaining egg whites. Stir in the hot sauce, nutmeg, salt and pepper. Pour evenly into the prepared ramekins.

Arrange the ramekins in a baking pan. Add enough hot water to the baking pan to reach halfway up the sides of the ramekins. Bake for 16 minutes or until the soufflés rise and are golden brown. Serve immediately.

Cherry Streusel Coffee Cake

Serves 8

Streusel Topping

1 cup lightly packed brown sugar
1/4 cup sugar
2 1/2 ounces sliced almonds
1/4 cup (1/2 stick) unsalted butter or margarine

Coffee Cake

2 1/2 cups cake flour
1 tablespoon baking powder
1/2 teaspoon salt
1/2 cup (1 stick) unsalted butter or margarine, softened
3/4 cup sugar
1 egg
1 tablespoon vegetable oil
3/4 cup buttermilk
1/2 cup sour cream
1 teaspoon almond extract
1 (16-ounce) can red tart or sweet cherries, drained
Confectioners' sugar (optional)

*F*or the topping, combine the brown sugar, sugar and almonds in a bowl and mix well. Cut in the butter until crumbly.

For the coffee cake, preheat the oven to 375 degrees. Sift the cake flour, baking powder and salt together. Beat the butter and sugar in a mixing bowl until light and fluffy, scraping the bowl occasionally. Add the egg and oil and beat until blended. Beat in the buttermilk, sour cream and flavoring. Stir in the dry ingredients just until combined; do not overmix.

Spread the batter in a greased and floured 10-inch baking pan and top with the cherries. Sprinkle with the topping. Bake for 30 minutes or until puffed and golden brown. Cool and sprinkle with confectioners' sugar.

Chocolate Hazelnut Biscotti

Makes 30 biscotti

2 cups flour, sifted
1 cup sugar
1/2 teaspoon baking powder
1/2 teaspoon baking soda
1/4 teaspoon salt
2 cups (12 ounces) semisweet chocolate chips
3/4 cup coarsely chopped toasted hazelnuts
2 eggs
2 tablespoons milk
1 teaspoon vanilla extract
1/2 teaspoon almond extract (optional)

*P*reheat the oven to 375 degrees. Mix the flour, sugar, baking powder, baking soda and salt in a bowl. Stir in the chocolate chips and hazelnuts. Whisk the eggs, milk and flavorings in a bowl until blended. Add the egg mixture to the flour mixture and mix well. Turn onto a lightly floured surface and knead gently until the dough adheres.

Divide the dough into 2 equal portions and shape each portion into a 3×10-inch log with moist hands. Arrange the logs 3 inches apart on a baking sheet lined with baking parchment. Bake for 25 to 30 minutes or until brown, rotating the baking sheet after 15 minutes. Remove from the oven and reduce the oven temperature to 300 degrees.

Let the logs cool for 30 minutes. Cut the logs diagonally into 1/2-inch slices using a serrated knife. Arrange the slices cut side up on the baking sheet. Bake for 20 minutes or until light brown. Cool on the pan on a wire rack. Store in an airtight container.

Berry Crème Fraîche Scones with Lemon Glaze

Makes 1 dozen scones

Scones

2 cups flour

1/4 cup packed brown sugar

2 teaspoons baking powder

1 teaspoon cinnamon

1 teaspoon ginger

1/2 teaspoon salt

6 tablespoons (3/4 stick) unsalted butter,
   chilled and cut into pieces

1/3 cup dried cranberries

1/3 cup dried blueberries

1 egg yolk

1 egg

2/3 cup crème fraîche or sour cream, chilled

1 1/2 teaspoons vanilla extract

Lemon Glaze

2 cups confectioners' sugar

1/2 cup fresh lemon juice

Finely chopped zest of 1 lemon

1 tablespoon unsalted butter

*F*or the scones, preheat the oven to 350 degrees. Combine the flour, brown sugar, baking powder, cinnamon, ginger and salt in a bowl and mix well. Cut in the butter until crumbly. Stir in the cranberries and blueberries. Whisk the egg yolk, egg, crème fraîche and vanilla in a bowl until blended. Gently stir the crème fraîche mixture into the berry mixture; the dough will be very moist.

Turn the dough onto a generously floured hard surface and divide into 2 equal portions. Press each portion into a 6-inch round, about 1/2 inch thick. Cut each round into 6 wedges. Arrange the wedges on a baking sheet and bake for 25 minutes or until a wooden pick inserted in the center comes out clean. Remove to a wire rack to cool.

For the glaze, mix the confectioners' sugar and lemon juice in a microwave-safe bowl and stir until the confectioners' sugar dissolves. Stir in the lemon zest and butter. Microwave on High for 30 seconds and whisk until smooth. Drizzle the glaze over the scones.

Amaretto French Toast

Serves 1

2 thin slices challah or egg bread
2 tablespoons cream cheese, softened
2 tablespoons marmalade or fruit preserves
1 cup milk

1 egg, beaten
1 to 2 tablespoons amaretto
Cinnamon to taste
1 to 2 tablespoons butter

Spread 1 side of 1 slice of the bread with the cream cheese. Spread 1 side of the remaining slice of bread with the marmalade and press together to form a sandwich. Whisk the milk, egg, liqueur and cinnamon in a shallow dish and dip the sandwich in the egg mixture. Brown in the butter in a skillet for 3 to 4 minutes per side, turning once. Serve with additional butter and warm syrup.

Sour Cream Cinnamon Twists

Makes 2 dozen twists

2 1/4 teaspoons dry yeast
1/4 cup warm water
4 cups flour
1 cup sour cream
1 cup (2 sticks) butter, melted

2 eggs
1 teaspoon salt
1 teaspoon vanilla extract
1 cup sugar
1 teaspoon cinnamon

Dissolve the yeast in the warm water in a large mixing bowl. Add the flour, sour cream, butter, eggs, salt, and vanilla to the yeast mixture and beat until smooth. Chill, covered, for 2 hours or for up to 2 days.

Preheat the oven to 375 degrees. Mix the sugar and cinnamon in a bowl and sprinkle 1/2 cup of the sugar mixture onto a hard surface. Roll the dough into a 15×18-inch rectangle on the prepared surface. Turn the rectangle and coat the remaining side with the sugar mixture. Fold the rectangle 3 times, like a letter, and roll 1/4 inch thick. Cut the rectangle into 1×4-inch strips. Twist each strip and arrange on a greased baking sheet. Sprinkle the twists with the remaining sugar mixture and bake for 15 minutes. Cool on the baking sheet for 2 minutes and remove to a wire rack to cool completely. Store the twists in an airtight container.

Sticky Buns

Makes 40 buns

Dough
2 (1/4-ounce) packages dry yeast
1 tablespoon sugar
1 cup lukewarm water
1 cup milk
5 tablespoons shortening
1/2 cup sugar
1 teaspoon salt
7 cups sifted flour
3 eggs, beaten

Filling
1 1/2 cups packed brown sugar
1 tablespoon cinnamon

Syrup and Assembly
2 cups packed brown sugar
1/2 cup (1 stick) plus 7 tablespoons butter
1 (16-ounce) bottle light corn syrup
10 ounces pecan halves
6 tablespoons butter, melted

For the dough, dissolve the yeast and 1 tablespoon sugar in the lukewarm water. Scald the milk in a saucepan over low heat; do not boil. Remove from the heat and add the shortening, 1/2 cup sugar and salt. Stir until the shortening melts and cool to lukewarm.

Add 2 cups of the flour to the milk mixture and mix well. Stir in the yeast mixture and eggs. Add just enough of the remaining 5 cups of flour to make a soft dough and mix well. Knead lightly and place the dough in a greased bowl, turning to coat the surface. Let rise, covered, in a warm place free from drafts for 1 to 1 1/2 hours or until doubled in bulk.

For the filling, mix the brown sugar and cinnamon in a bowl.

For the syrup, combine the brown sugar, butter and corn syrup in a saucepan. Cook over low heat until blended, stirring constantly. Pour the syrup equally into two 9×13-inch baking pans, tilting the pans to ensure even coverage. Sprinkle the pecans over the prepared layers.

To assemble, punch the dough down and divide into 2 equal portions. Roll each portion into a rectangle on a lightly floured surface. Brush each rectangle with 3 tablespoons of the melted butter and sprinkle evenly with the filling. Roll as for a jelly roll and cut each roll into about 20 slices.

Arrange the slices cut side up in the prepared pans. Let rise, covered with plastic wrap, until doubled in bulk. Preheat the oven to 375 degrees and bake for 25 minutes. Invert the buns onto a foil-lined baking sheet.

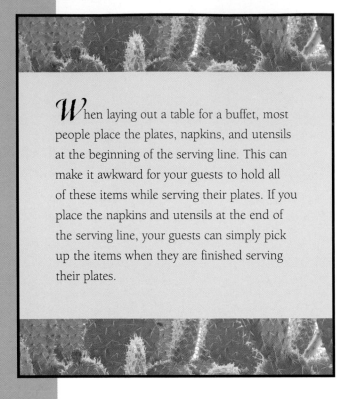

When laying out a table for a buffet, most people place the plates, napkins, and utensils at the beginning of the serving line. This can make it awkward for your guests to hold all of these items while serving their plates. If you place the napkins and utensils at the end of the serving line, your guests can simply pick up the items when they are finished serving their plates.

Lemon Crème Brûlée

Serves 6

2 cups cream
6 egg yolks
2 eggs
1 cup sugar
1/4 cup fresh lemon juice
Grated zest of 2 lemons
Sugar to taste
Lemon zest, fresh blueberries or fresh raspberries

Preheat the oven to 350 degrees. Heat the cream in a saucepan over medium heat just until hot; do not scald. Whisk the egg yolks and eggs in a bowl until smooth. Add 1 cup sugar to the eggs gradually, whisking constantly until blended. Stir in the lemon juice and lemon zest. Add the warm cream gradually, whisking constantly.

Pour the lemon mixture into six 6-ounce ramekins and arrange the ramekins in a large baking pan. Add enough hot water to the baking pan to reach halfway up the sides of the ramekins. Bake for 25 minutes. Remove to a wire rack to cool.

Sprinkle the top of each crème brûlée lightly with sugar to taste. Caramelize the sugar with a culinary torch. Garnish with additional lemon zest, fresh blueberries or fresh raspberries.

Chocolate Coffee Bean Cheesecake

Serves 10 to 12

Chocolate Coffee Bean Crust
6 ounces chocolate wafer cookies
1/4 cup (1/2 stick) butter, melted
1/4 cup ground or crushed coffee beans (espresso or chocolate macadamia)

Nutty Cream Cheese Filling
16 ounces cream cheese, softened
2/3 cup sugar
1 egg
1/2 cup sour cream
1/4 cup crushed chocolate-covered nuts
2 teaspoons vanilla extract

Creamy Coffee Topping
1 cup sugar
1/2 cup brewed coffee
1 cup vanilla yogurt

*F*or the crust, preheat the oven to 350 degrees. Process the cookies in a food processor until finely ground. The cookie crumbs should measure about 1 1/2 cups. Mix the crumbs and butter in a bowl and press over the bottom and 1/2 inch up the side of a 9-inch springform pan with a removable side. Bake for 10 minutes. Cool and sprinkle with the coffee beans. Maintain the oven temperature.

For the filling, beat the cream cheese and sugar in a mixing bowl until smooth, scraping the bowl occasionally. Add the egg and beat until blended. Beat in the sour cream, nuts and vanilla. Spread the filling over the beans. Bake for 30 minutes or until the center barely jiggles when gently shaken. Remove from the oven and run a sharp knife around the edge of the filling. Cool slightly and chill for 3 hours or for up to 2 days.

For the topping, combine the sugar and coffee in a saucepan and cook until of a syrup consistency, stirring frequently. Remove from the heat and cool. Combine 2 tablespoons of the syrup and the yogurt in a bowl and mix well. Spread over the top of the cheesecake. Remove the side and cut into wedges. Reserve the remaining coffee syrup for other recipes.

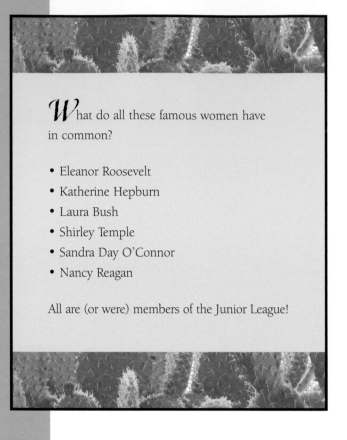

Cream Cheese Pound Cake

Serves 16

1¹/2 cups (3 sticks) butter, softened
8 ounces cream cheese, softened
3 cups sugar
1 tablespoon vanilla extract
6 eggs
3 cups flour

*P*reheat the oven to 325 degrees. Combine the butter, cream cheese, sugar and vanilla in a mixing bowl. Beat at medium-high speed for 2 minutes or until light and fluffy; scrape the side of the bowl. Add the eggs 1 at a time, beating at medium speed for 10 seconds after each addition and scraping the bowl. Beat for 30 seconds longer. Gently stir in the flour with a rubber spatula. Beat at low speed for 5 seconds. Scrape the side of the bowl and beat for 5 to 10 seconds longer or until smooth.

Spoon the batter into a lightly buttered 10-inch tube pan and place the pan on the center oven rack. Bake for 1 hour and 35 minutes or until golden brown and a wooden pick inserted in the center comes out clean. Cool in the pan on a wire rack and invert onto a cake plate.

Tartes aux Pommes with Caramel

Serves 6

1 sheet frozen puff pastry, thawed
2 Golden Delicious apples
3 tablespoons sugar
1 teaspoon cinnamon
3 tablespoons unsalted butter, melted
Caramel sauce or honey

*L*ine 2 baking sheets with baking parchment. Roll the pastry into a 14×18-inch rectangle on a lightly floured surface. Cut out six 5-inch rounds with a small plate or round cutter. Place 3 rounds on each baking sheet. Chill, covered, for 30 minutes or for up to 8 hours.

Position 1 oven rack in the top third of the oven and 1 oven rack in the bottom third of the oven. Preheat the oven to 400 degrees. Peel the apples and cut into halves. Cut each half into thin slices. Overlap the apples slices to within 1/4 inch of the edge of each round. Sprinkle with 3/4 of the sugar and the cinnamon and drizzle with 3/4 of the butter. Brush the edges with the remaining butter and sprinkle with the remaining sugar. Bake for 25 minutes or until the pastry is brown and the apples are tender.

To serve, drizzle caramel sauce in a decorative pattern on 6 dessert plates. Arrange 1 tart on each plate and drizzle with additional caramel sauce if desired. Or, sprinkle with confectioners' sugar and top with a scoop of ice cream.

The Valley of the Sun is one of the few areas in the country to boast professional teams in all major sports. The Arizona Diamondbacks, Arizona Cardinals, Phoenix Coyotes, and Phoenix Suns, as well as Arizona Rattlers and Phoenix Mercury, all call the Valley home. The area is also home to Cactus League Spring Training, where you can catch a baseball game nearly every afternoon in March at a handful of stadiums. College sports are popular as well, with Arizona State University just minutes away from Phoenix. The city of Tempe hosts the Tostitos Fiesta Bowl played at ASU's Sun Devil Stadium. Any sporting event is more fun when shared with friends and delicious food, no matter which team you're rooting for.

Fan Fare

Cocktails
Fog Cutter
Mai Tai
Game Day Sangria

Appetizers
Tamari-Roasted Almonds
Prosciutto-Wrapped Asparagus
Stuffed Mushrooms
Warm Herbed Olives
Artichoke and Blue Cheese Dip
Friendship Cup Soup

Salads and Sandwiches
Three-Leaf Salad with Mandarin Oranges and
    Feta Cheese
Wine-Baked Turkey and Wild Rice Salad
Shrimp, Mango and Black Bean Salad
Roast Chicken Panini
Grilled Pork Tenderloin Sandwiches

Sides
Grilled Corn with Chili Butter and Lime
Green Chile Corn Casserole
Beet and Potato Salad
Garlic-Grilled Tomatoes

Main Courses
Blue Cheese-Stuffed Hamburgers
Enchilada Bake
Lamb and Eggplant Pastitsio
Ahi Tuna Burgers with Ginger Mustard Glaze
Shrimp Fettuccini

Desserts
Earthquake Cake
Kahlúa Cake
Majorette Brownies
Camelback Mountain Cookies

Fan Fare

tailgates, barbecues, and potlucks

Prosciutto-Wrapped Asparagus

Serves 8 to 10

2 bunches asparagus
Salt to taste
4 ounces prosciutto, thinly sliced
4 ounces boursin or allouette

*S*nap off the woody ends of the asparagus spears. Bring 1¹/2 inches of salted water to a boil in a deep skillet. Add the asparagus to the boiling water and cook for 2 minutes or until tender-crisp. Drain in a colander and rinse with cold water. Pat dry with paper towels.

Cut each slice of prosciutto lengthwise into 1-inch strips. Spread 1 side of each strip with about ¹/2 teaspoon of the cheese. Wrap each strip, cheese side in, in a spiral pattern around an asparagus spear, trimming the excess. Arrange the wrapped asparagus spears in a decorative pattern on a serving platter.

Stuffed Mushrooms

Makes 20 stuffed mushrooms

1 pound fresh mushrooms, stems removed
6 tablespoons (³/4 stick) unsalted
   butter, melted
8 ounces cream cheese, softened
³/4 cup (3 ounces) grated Parmesan cheese

3 tablespoons milk
2 teaspoons chopped fresh chives
2 teaspoons chopped fresh flat-leaf parsley
¹/4 teaspoon hot sauce, or to taste

*P*reheat the oven to 350 degrees. Brush the surface of the mushroom caps with the butter and arrange stem side up on a baking sheet.

Beat the cream cheese, Parmesan cheese, milk, chives, parsley and hot sauce in a mixing bowl until combined. Spoon some of cream cheese mixture into each mushroom cap. You may prepare to this point up to 4 hours in advance and store, covered, in the refrigerator. Bake for 20 minutes and serve immediately.

Warm Herbed Olives

Serves 4

1/4 cup extra-virgin olive oil
3 garlic cloves, thinly sliced
2 sprigs of fresh thyme, or 1/4 teaspoon
  dried thyme

1 cup drained pitted kalamata or niçoise
  olives, or a mixture of different types
  of olives

Combine the olive oil, garlic and thyme in a small saucepan and mix well. Cook over low heat for 2 to 3 minutes or until the garlic is fragrant. Stir in the olives. Cook for 2 to 3 minutes longer or until heated through, stirring occasionally. Pour into a serving bowl and serve warm. For variety, serve with creamy goat cheese and crusty French bread to soak up the olive oil mixture. Or, purée to make a tapenade.

Artichoke and Blue Cheese Dip

Serves 6

6 slices bacon, chopped
2 garlic cloves, minced
8 ounces cream cheese, softened
1/4 cup half-and-half
1 cup (4 ounces) crumbled blue cheese
1 (8-ounce) can quartered artichokes, drained
  and chopped

1 (5-ounce) can water chestnuts, drained
  and chopped
2 tablespoons chopped fresh chives
1 teaspoon hot sauce, or to taste
3 tablespoons chopped smoked almonds
2 tablespoons chopped fresh chives

Cook the bacon in a large skillet over medium-high heat for 7 minutes or until almost crisp; drain the excess fat. Add the garlic to the skillet and sauté for 2 to 3 minutes. Preheat the oven to 350 degrees.

Beat the cream cheese in a mixing bowl until light and fluffy. Add the half-and-half and beat until blended. Stir in the bacon mixture, blue cheese, artichokes, water chestnuts, 2 tablespoons chives and hot sauce. Taste and adjust the seasonings.

Spread the cream cheese mixture in a baking dish. Bake, covered with foil, for 30 minutes or until bubbly. Sprinkle with the almonds and 2 tablespoons chives. Serve with sliced apples, celery sticks, sliced French bread and/or assorted party crackers. You may prepare in advance and store, covered, in the refrigerator or freeze for future use. Bring to room temperature before reheating.

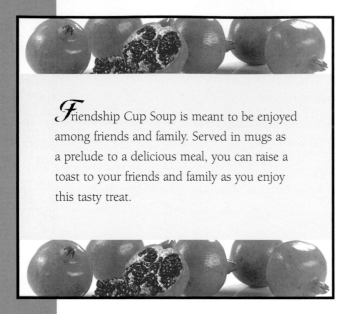

Friendship Cup Soup is meant to be enjoyed among friends and family. Served in mugs as a prelude to a delicious meal, you can raise a toast to your friends and family as you enjoy this tasty treat.

Friendship Cup Soup

Transport to a football game in a thermos on a cold day.

Serves 2 to 3

1 (10-ounce) can tomato soup
1 (10-ounce) can beef broth
1 soup can water
1/4 teaspoon marjoram
1/4 teaspoon thyme

*C*ombine the soup, broth, water, marjoram and thyme in a saucepan and mix well. Simmer for 2 minutes, stirring occasionally. Ladle into mugs and serve immediately.

Three-Leaf Salad with Mandarin Oranges and Feta Cheese

Serves 8 to 10

Poppy Sesame Dressing
1 cup vegetable oil
1/3 cup cider vinegar
1/4 cup sugar
1 teaspoon grated onion
1 teaspoon dry mustard
1 teaspoon poppy seeds
1 teaspoon sesame seeds

Salad
1 head romaine, trimmed and torn
1 head red leaf lettuce, trimmed and torn
1 bunch spinach, trimmed and torn
8 ounces bacon, crisp-cooked and crumbled
2 cups drained canned mandarin oranges
11/2 cups (6 ounces) crumbled feta cheese
1/2 red onion, thinly sliced

*F*or the dressing, combine the oil, vinegar, sugar, onion, dry mustard, poppy seeds and sesame seeds in a jar with a tight-fitting lid and seal tightly. Shake to mix.

For the salad, toss the romaine, leaf lettuce, spinach, bacon, oranges, cheese and onion in a bowl. Add the dressing and mix until coated. Serve immediately.

Wine-Baked Turkey and Wild Rice Salad

Serves 4 to 6

Lemon Ginger Vinaigrette
2/3 cup vegetable oil
1/4 cup rice vinegar
1/4 cup fresh lemon juice
2 teaspoons minced fresh gingerroot
1 teaspoon soy sauce
1/2 teaspoon pepper
1/4 teaspoon salt

Salad
1/2 turkey breast
2 tablespoons butter

1/2 cup white wine
1/4 cup water
1/2 cup long grain white rice
1 cup hot water
1/2 teaspoon salt
1/2 cup wild rice
1 1/2 cups baby peas
1/2 cup golden raisins
4 green onions, minced
1/4 cup slivered almonds, toasted

*F*or the vinaigrette, combine the oil, vinegar, lemon juice, gingerroot, soy sauce, pepper and salt in a jar with a tight-fitting lid and seal tightly. Shake to mix.

For the salad, preheat the oven to 350 degrees. Brown the turkey on all sides in the butter in an ovenproof skillet. Add the wine and 1/4 cup water to the skillet and bake, covered, for 30 to 45 minutes or until a meat thermometer registers 170 degrees. Let stand until cool.

Combine the white rice, hot water and salt in a saucepan and mix well. Steam for 20 minutes. Remove from the heat and let stand, covered, for 15 minutes. Cook the wild rice using the package directions. Drain and stir into the white rice.

Blanch the peas in boiling water in a saucepan for 2 minutes; drain. Cut the turkey into bite-size pieces and combine with the rice mixture, peas, raisins, green onions and almonds in a bowl. Add the vinaigrette and toss to coat.

Shrimp, Mango and Black Bean Salad

Serves 6

3 cups drained canned black beans, rinsed
2 garlic cloves, minced
2 mangoes, peeled and chopped
1 red bell pepper, chopped
1/2 avocado, chopped
1/2 red onion, chopped
1 to 2 tablespoons chopped jalapeño chiles
1/2 cup lime juice
1/4 cup chopped fresh cilantro
2 tablespoons sour cream
1 tablespoon cumin
1 tablespoon chili powder
1 teaspoon coriander
1 teaspoon oregano
1 pound (16- to 20-count) medium shrimp, peeled and deveined
2 tablespoons olive oil or butter
Salt and pepper to taste
5 ounces lettuce leaves or baby spinach leaves

Combine the beans and garlic in a bowl and mix well. Stir in the mangoes, bell pepper, avocado, onion and jalapeño chiles. Combine the lime juice, cilantro, sour cream, cumin, chili powder, coriander and oregano in a bowl and mix well. Add to the bean mixture and toss to mix.

Sauté the shrimp in the olive oil in a large skillet for 5 to 6 minutes or until the shrimp turn pink. Add the shrimp to the bean mixture and toss to mix. Season with salt and pepper. Spoon the salad onto lettuce-lined serving plates.

Roast Chicken Panini

Serves 4

1 roasted chicken
1 tablespoon extra-virgin olive oil
1 tablespoon butter
1 onion, chopped
8 thin slices crusty Italian bread
1 pound fontina cheese, shredded or sliced
1 medium jar roasted red and yellow bell peppers, drained
Extra-virgin olive oil to taste

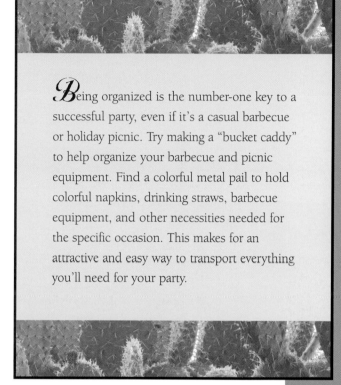

Being organized is the number-one key to a successful party, even if it's a casual barbecue or holiday picnic. Try making a "bucket caddy" to help organize your barbecue and picnic equipment. Find a colorful metal pail to hold colorful napkins, drinking straws, barbecue equipment, and other necessities needed for the specific occasion. This makes for an attractive and easy way to transport everything you'll need for your party.

Shred the chicken, discarding the skin and bones. Heat a small skillet over medium to medium-high heat and add 1 tablespoon olive oil and the butter to the hot skillet. Add the onion and sauté for 10 to 12 minutes or until caramelized.

Preheat a large grill pan or griddle pan over medium to medium-high heat. Arrange 4 of the bread slices on a hard surface. Layer each slice with a thin layer of the cheese, shredded chicken, 1/4 of the onion and 1/4 of the roasted bell peppers. Top with the remaining bread slices, forming a sandwich.

Drizzle 1 side of each sandwich with additional olive oil and arrange oil side down in the preheated grill pan. Drizzle the remaining side with additional olive oil. Weight down the sandwiches with foil-wrapped bricks or a heavy skillet weighted with a sack of flour or canned goods. Cook for 2 to 3 minutes per side, turning once. Serve immediately.

Grilled Pork Tenderloin Sandwiches

Makes 6 to 8 sandwiches

Mustard Sauce
1/2 cup Dijon mustard
1/4 cup olive oil
1 garlic clove, crushed
1 tablespoon soy sauce
1/2 teaspoon rosemary

Sandwiches
1 (11/2-pound) pork tenderloin
1 (4-ounce) tub garlic and herb cream cheese
1 tablespoon Dijon mustard
1 loaf sourdough bread
4 ounces Swiss cheese, sliced
1 (7-ounce) jar roasted red bell peppers, drained, split and seeds removed
Spinach leaves
Sliced red onion

*F*or the sauce, combine the mustard, olive oil, garlic, soy sauce and rosemary in a bowl and mix well.

For the sandwiches, preheat the grill. Grill the pork using the package directions until a meat thermometer registers 160 degrees for medium, basting with the sauce occasionally; do not overcook. The pork should be slightly pink when removed from the grill. Cover the pork loosely with foil and allow to rest before slicing.

Combine the cream cheese and mustard in a bowl and mix well. Slice the bread loaf horizontally into halves. Spread the cream cheese mixture over the cut sides of the halves. Layer the bottom half with sliced pork, cheese, roasted bell peppers, spinach and onion and top with the remaining bread half cream cheese side down. Cut the loaf diagonally into 6 to 8 sandwiches.

Grilled Corn with Chili Butter and Lime

Serves 4

Chili Butter
1/4 cup (1/2 stick) unsalted
   butter, softened
1 tablespoon chili powder
1/4 teaspoon salt
1/4 teaspoon ground pepper

Corn
4 ears unhusked yellow or
   white corn
2 limes, cut into quarters
2 tablespoons minced
   fresh cilantro

*F*or the butter, combine the butter, chili powder, salt and pepper in a bowl and mix well.

For the corn, pull the corn husks back on each ear, leaving the husks attached at the base of the cob. Remove the silk and reposition the husks. Soak the corn in a large container of water for 2 hours or longer; drain on a tea towel. Preheat the grill. Pull the husks down and spread 1 tablespoon of the butter over each ear. Reposition the husks and tie the ends if necessary. Grill the corn over hot coals for 20 minutes or until the kernels are tender, turning occasionally. Pull the husks back and arrange the corn on a platter. Squeeze with the limes and sprinkle with the cilantro. Serve immediately.

The Phoenix Affiliate was created in October 1999, but the Komen Phoenix Race for the Cure® celebrated its eleventh year in 2003. Three friends and members of The Junior League of Phoenix determined in 1992 after the loss of one of their friends to breast cancer that something needed to be done to fight this disease. They joined forces with Banner Health (then known as Samaritan Health System) to bring Race for the Cure® to Phoenix for the first time in 1993.

Green Chile Corn Casserole

Serves 8 to 10

1 garlic clove, minced
1/2 cup (1 stick) unsalted butter
4 cups sour cream
1 (8-ounce) package corn bread mix
1 (8-ounce) package yellow cake mix

2 (15-ounce) cans cream-style corn
2 (4-ounce) cans chopped green chiles
4 eggs, lightly beaten
2 tablespoons chili powder

*P*reheat the oven to 350 degrees. Sweat the garlic in the butter in a sauté pan. Combine the garlic, sour cream, corn bread mix, cake mix, corn, green chiles, eggs and chili powder in a bowl and mix well. The mixture will be very sweet. Cut the sweetness by adding salt or hot sauce if desired. Spoon the corn mixture into a 9×13-inch baking pan and bake for 60 to 80 minutes or until brown and bubbly. Omit the green chiles for just a corn casserole.

Beet and Potato Salad

Serves 6 to 8

6 potatoes (about 2 pounds)
1 cup mayonnaise
1 (15-ounce) can sliced beets, drained and chopped
3 tablespoons olive oil
Salt and pepper to taste

*C*ombine the potatoes with enough water to cover in a saucepan. Bring to a boil and reduce the heat. Simmer, covered, for 20 to 25 minutes or until tender. Drain and let stand until cool. Peel and coarsely chop the potatoes.

Combine the potatoes and mayonnaise in a bowl and mix gently. Stir in the beets. Add the olive oil and toss to coat. Season with salt and pepper and chill, covered, until serving time.

Garlic-Grilled Tomatoes

Serves 6

6 ripe red tomatoes
Salt and pepper to taste
6 garlic cloves, minced
3 tablespoons olive oil
2 ounces Parmigiano-Reggiano cheese, grated
2 tablespoons fresh thyme leaves

*P*reheat the grill. Cut the tomatoes horizontally into halves. Sprinkle the cut sides with salt and pepper. Sauté the garlic in the olive oil in a skillet over medium heat for 1 to 2 minutes. Remove from the heat and reserve.

Arrange the tomatoes cut side down on the hot grill rack and grill for 3 to 5 minutes or until light brown. Turn the tomato halves with tongs and drizzle about 1 1/2 teaspoons of the reserved garlic oil over each half. Grill for 3 to 5 minutes longer or until the bottoms are brown. Remove the tomatoes to a platter and sprinkle with the cheese and thyme. Serve immediately.

Blue Cheese-Stuffed Hamburgers

Serves 4

Special Seasoning

2^1/$_2$ tablespoons Hungarian paprika

2 tablespoons salt

1 tablespoon black pepper

1 tablespoon cumin

1 tablespoon cayenne pepper

1 tablespoon leaf oregano

1 tablespoon thyme

1 tablespoon parsley flakes

Hamburgers

1 tablespoon minced garlic

1 teaspoon salt

^{1}/$_2$ teaspoon ground pepper

2 pounds ground chuck

8 ounces blue cheese

4 large whole wheat buns, split

Sliced tomatoes

Romaine lettuce

Grilled sliced onions

*F*or the seasoning, combine the paprika, salt, black pepper, cumin, cayenne pepper, oregano, thyme and parsley flakes in a small bowl and mix well. Store in an airtight container.

For the hamburgers, preheat the grill. Mix 1 teaspoon of the seasoning, the garlic, salt and pepper in a bowl. Sprinkle the seasoning mixture over the ground chuck in a bowl and mix just until distributed. Divide the ground chuck mixture into 8 equal portions and shape each portion into a patty.

Crumble the cheese into a bowl and shape into 4 equal patties. Arrange 1 cheese patty on each of 4 beef patties. Top with the remaining beef patties. Grill the stuffed patties over hot coals until a meat thermometer registers 160 degrees, or, if desired, cook in a large skillet over medium-high heat until the patties are cooked through. Arrange the buns cut side down on the grill rack and grill for 30 seconds or just until heated through. Remove the patties and buns from the grill and serve with sliced tomatoes, lettuce and grilled onions.

Enchilada Bake

Serves 8

2 pounds ground beef, ground turkey or soy crumbles
1 onion, chopped
1 garlic clove, minced
2 tablespoons chili powder
2 teaspoons paprika
2 teaspoons cumin
3 cups tomato sauce or tomato purée
1 (4-ounce) can chopped green chiles
1/2 cup chopped black olives
1 tablespoon salt
1 teaspoon sugar
12 corn tortillas
Vegetable oil
2 cups small curd cottage cheese
1 egg, beaten
8 ounces Monterey Jack cheese, shredded
1 cup (4 ounces) shredded Cheddar cheese
Sour cream

*B*rown the ground beef in a skillet, stirring until crumbly; drain. Add the onion and garlic to the ground beef and cook until the onion is tender, stirring frequently. Sprinkle with the chili powder, paprika and cumin. Stir in the tomato sauce, green chiles, olives, salt and sugar. Simmer for 15 minutes, stirring occasionally.

Preheat the oven to 350 degrees. Soften the tortillas in a small amount of oil in a skillet and drain on paper towels. Mix the cottage cheese and egg in a bowl. Layer 1/3 of the ground beef mixture, 1/2 of the Monterey Jack cheese, 1/2 of the cottage cheese mixture and 1/2 of the tortillas in a 9×13-inch baking dish. Top with 1/2 of the remaining ground beef mixture, the remaining Monterey Jack cheese, remaining cottage cheese mixture, remaining tortillas and remaining ground beef mixture. Sprinkle with the Cheddar cheese and bake for 30 minutes. Garnish with sour cream.

Lamb and Eggplant Pastitsio

Serves 6 to 8

Lamb Sauce

1 large onion, chopped
1 tablespoon olive oil
1 pound lean ground lamb
1 garlic clove, minced
1 tablespoon sugar
1 1/2 teaspoons salt
1 teaspoon oregano
1 teaspoon cumin
1/2 teaspoon cinnamon
1/4 teaspoon pepper
1 (1-pound) eggplant, peeled and cut into
    1/2-inch pieces
1 (28- to 32-ounce) can crushed tomatoes
Salt and pepper to taste

Cheese Sauce

2 tablespoons unsalted butter
2 tablespoons flour
2 cups milk
1 garlic clove
1 whole clove
8 ounces feta cheese, crumbled
1/2 teaspoon salt
1/4 teaspoon pepper
2 eggs

Pasta and Assembly

10 ounces penne
Salt to taste
1 cup (4 ounces) grated Parmesan cheese

*F*or the lamb sauce, cook the onion in the olive oil in a 4-quart heavy saucepan over medium heat for 3 to 5 minutes or until tender, stirring constantly. Add the lamb and sauté over high heat for 5 minutes or until the lamb is no longer pink, stirring and breaking up clumps. Stir in the garlic, sugar, 1 1/2 teaspoons salt, oregano, cumin, cinnamon and 1/4 teaspoon pepper and sauté for 2 minutes. Stir the eggplant and undrained tomatoes into the lamb mixture. Simmer, covered, for 40 minutes or just until the eggplant is tender, stirring occasionally; remove the cover. Simmer for 15 minutes longer or until thickened, stirring occasionally. Season with salt and pepper to taste.

For the cheese sauce, melt the butter in a 2-quart saucepan over medium heat. Add the flour and stir until smooth. Cook for 2 minutes, stirring constantly. Whisk in the milk until blended and add the garlic clove and whole clove. Bring to a boil, whisking constantly; reduce the heat. Simmer for 5 minutes, whisking occasionally. Stir in the cheese, salt and pepper. Cook until blended, whisking constantly. Discard the garlic clove and whole clove. Whisk the eggs in a bowl until blended. Stir a small amount of the hot sauce into the eggs and stir the eggs into the hot sauce.

For the pasta and assembly, preheat the oven to 425 degrees. Cook the pasta in boiling salted water in a saucepan until al dente and drain. Toss 1/2 of the pasta with the lamb sauce and toss the remaining pasta with the cheese sauce. Spread the lamb sauce mixture in a shallow 3-quart baking dish. Spoon the cheese sauce mixture over the prepared layer and sprinkle with the cheese. Bake on the middle oven rack for 25 to 30 minutes or until brown and bubbly. Let stand for 5 minutes.

Ahi Tuna Burgers with Ginger Mustard Glaze

Serves 4

Ginger Mustard Glaze

2/3 cup teriyaki sauce

2 tablespoons honey

2 tablespoons Dijon mustard

4 teaspoons minced fresh gingerroot

2 teaspoons Sriracha Hot Chili Sauce

1 teaspoon minced garlic

1 teaspoon red wine vinegar

Tuna Burgers

1 1/2 pounds Ahi tuna, skin and
  gristle removed

1 egg, beaten

3 tablespoons Dijon mustard

2 teaspoons minced garlic

1 teaspoon kosher salt

1/2 teaspoon cayenne pepper

1/4 teaspoon freshly ground black pepper

1/4 cup olive oil

1 to 2 tablespoons butter

4 hamburger buns with sesame seeds, split

1/4 cup sliced Japanese pickled ginger
  (optional)

*F*or the glaze, combine the teriyaki sauce, honey, mustard, gingerroot, chili sauce, garlic and vinegar in a saucepan and mix well. Bring to a boil; reduce the heat. Simmer for 5 minutes or until thickened, stirring frequently. Strain into a heatproof bowl, discarding the solids, and cover to keep warm. You may prepare up to 2 days in advance and store, covered, in the refrigerator. Reheat before serving.

For the burgers, have the butcher grind the tuna. If this is not an option, grind the tuna in a meat grinder or chop with a sharp knife until the texture of ground meat. Do not use a food processor. Combine the tuna, egg, mustard, garlic, salt, cayenne pepper and black pepper in a bowl and mix well. Divide the tuna mixture into 4 equal portions and shape each portion into a patty. Chill, covered with plastic wrap, for 1 hour.

Heat the olive oil in a large skillet over medium-high heat. Sear the tuna patties in the hot oil for 3 to 4 minutes per side or until brown and medium-rare. Drain and cover to keep warm. Preheat the broiler. Spread the butter on the cut sides of the buns and arrange butter side up on a baking sheet. Broil until light brown.

To serve, arrange 1 tuna burger on the bottom half of each bun. Drizzle with 1 tablespoon of the warm glaze and sprinkle with some of the pickled ginger. Top with the remaining bun halves.

Shrimp Fettuccini

Serves 4

9 ounces fresh fettuccini
1 small onion, chopped
1/2 cup (1 stick) margarine
8 ounces Mexican Velveeta cheese, cubed
1 (10-ounce) can cream of mushroom soup
1 (1-pound) package thawed frozen shrimp, boiled shrimp
or crawfish tails
8 ounces Cheddar cheese, shredded

*P*reheat the oven to 350 degrees. Cook the pasta using the package directions until al dente, omitting the salt; drain. Sauté the onion in the margarine in a skillet until tender. Add the Velveeta cheese and cook until the cheese melts, stirring frequently. Stir in the soup and shrimp. Add the pasta and mix well.

Spoon the shrimp mixture into a baking dish and sprinkle with the Cheddar cheese. Bake for 20 minutes or until bubbly. Serve with garlic bread.

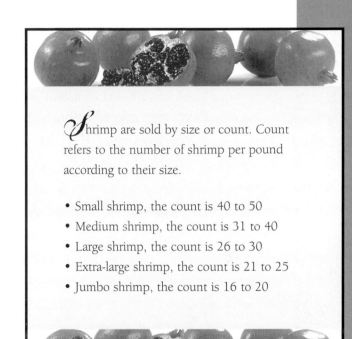

*S*hrimp are sold by size or count. Count refers to the number of shrimp per pound according to their size.

- Small shrimp, the count is 40 to 50
- Medium shrimp, the count is 31 to 40
- Large shrimp, the count is 26 to 30
- Extra-large shrimp, the count is 21 to 25
- Jumbo shrimp, the count is 16 to 20

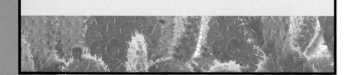

The day before you host a party, take out all the serving dishes, utensils, linens, and any other items that you will need for your table. Set out everything on the table the way that you plan to present it for the party. Label each serving dish with a small piece of paper stating what food will go in the dish. This will allow you to present a beautiful table to your guests and save you from rushing around as your guests arrive.

Earthquake Cake

Serves 10

1 cup shredded coconut
1 cup chopped nuts
1 (2-layer) package chocolate cake mix
1 cup (6 ounces) semisweet chocolate chips
8 ounces cream cheese, softened
1 (16-ounce) package confectioners' sugar
1/2 cup (1 stick) butter, melted

Preheat the oven to 350 degrees. Combine the coconut and nuts in a bowl and mix well. Press the coconut mixture over the bottom of a 9×13-inch cake pan. Prepare the cake mix using the package directions and stir in the chocolate chips. Spoon the batter into the prepared pan.

Beat the cream cheese, confectioners' sugar and butter in a mixing bowl until creamy, scraping the bowl occasionally. Drop or spread the cream cheese mixture evenly over the prepared layers. Bake for 45 to 60 minutes or until the edges pull away from the sides of the pan. Cool in the pan on a wire rack.

Kahlúa Cake

The flavor of the cake is even better a day or two after being baked.

Serves 16

Cake
1 (2-layer) package chocolate cake mix
2 eggs
1/3 cup Kahlúa
1/4 cup vegetable oil
1 (4-ounce) package vanilla instant pudding mix
2 cups sour cream
2 cups (12 ounces) semisweet chocolate chips

Kahlúa Glaze
1/2 cup confectioners' sugar
1/4 cup Kahlúa
Confectioners' sugar to taste

*F*or the cake, preheat the oven to 350 degrees. Combine the cake mix, eggs, liqueur, oil, pudding mix and sour cream in a bowl and mix by hand until blended. Stir in the chocolate chips and spoon the batter into a greased and floured bundt pan.

Bake for 45 to 50 minutes or until the cake tests done. Cool in the pan on a wire rack for 30 minutes. Invert onto a cake plate.

For the glaze, combine 1/2 cup confectioners' sugar and the liqueur in a bowl and stir until of a glaze consistency. Drizzle the glaze over the cooled cake and let stand until set. Sprinkle with confectioners' sugar to taste.

Majorette Brownies

Makes 16 brownies

1 1/4 cups flour
1 teaspoon baking powder
1/2 teaspoon salt
2 eggs
1 cup packed light brown sugar
1 teaspoon vanilla extract
1 cup (6 ounces) chocolate chips
1 1/2 cups chopped walnuts or pecans

*P*reheat the oven to 350 degrees. Mix the flour, baking powder and salt together. Whisk the eggs in a bowl until blended and stir in the brown sugar and vanilla. Add the flour mixture and mix well; the batter will be stiff. Stir in the chocolate chips and walnuts.

Spoon the batter into a greased 8×8-inch baking pan. Bake for 25 to 35 minutes or until the brownies test done. Cool in the pan on a wire rack and cut into squares. You may double the recipe and bake in a 9×13-inch baking pan.

Camelback Mountain Cookies

Indulge in one of these delicious cookies before an invigorating hike up Camelback Mountain, one of Phoenix's most popular hiking areas.

Makes 4 dozen cookies

6 cups rolled oats
2¹/2 teaspoons baking soda
1¹/2 cups sugar
1¹/2 cups packed brown sugar
¹/2 cup (1 stick) butter, softened, or
    butter-flavor shortening
4 eggs
1 teaspoon vanilla extract
1 (19-ounce) jar peanut butter
1 cup (6 ounces) chocolate chips

*P*reheat the oven to 375 degrees. Mix the oats and baking soda in a small bowl. Beat the sugar, brown sugar and butter in a mixing bowl until creamy, scraping the bowl occasionally. Add the eggs and vanilla and beat until blended. Beat in the peanut butter until smooth. Add the oats mixture and beat until combined. Stir in the chocolate chips.

*B*utter should be at room temperature for most baking recipes, unless otherwise specified in the recipe. To bring butter to room temperature, leave on the kitchen counter for twenty to thirty minutes or until it "gives" when lightly touched. Butter left out too long that can be "squished" will make your cookies spread. Chill the dough after combining to alleviate this problem.

Drop by ice cream scoopfuls onto an ungreased cookie sheet and bake for 10 to 13 minutes or until light brown and just barely set; do not overbake. Cool on the cookie sheet for 1 minute and remove to a wire rack to cool completely. Store in an airtight container. Bake for 8 to 10 minutes for smaller cookies. You may freeze baked cookies for future use.

The spring season brings many changes to Phoenix and its surrounding communities. The Superstition Mountains that were once bare are now covered with colorful wildflowers and blooming prickly pear cacti. Homes throughout the Valley begin to open their windows to smell the fragrant orange tree blossoms that permeate the crisp morning air. Many are inspired to begin their "spring cleaning," which lends a hand to The Junior League of Phoenix's Annual Rummage Sale, a Valley tradition for more than sixty-five years. Spring also brings busier schedules for all lifestyles, making it fun to take time out to relax and enjoy a casual gathering with family and friends.

Spring on the Run

photo donated by The Desert Botanical Gardens
photo © Charles Coheen

Beverages
Banana, Peanut Butter and Chocolate Smoothie
Tropical Blend Smoothie
Very Berry Smoothie

Soups
Fish Stew à la Provençal
Crab Chowder
Spring Minestrone

Salads
Black-Eyed Pea and Hominy Salad
Strawberry Spinach Salad
Tortellini Salad
Pacific Rim Seafood Salad

Sides
Glazed Carrots
Portobello and Mushroom Brie Cups
Crisp Rosemary Roasted Potatoes
Cheddar Cheese Biscuits

Main Courses
Sesame Ginger Beef Stir-Fry
Curried Meatballs
Spring Leg of Lamb with Tomato and
         Herb Vinaigrette
Chicken Oporto
Chicken Pesto Pan Pizza
Baked Fish Italienne

Pastas
Gnocchi with Chicken, Sun-Dried Tomatoes,
         Gorgonzola and Pine Nuts
Seafood Pasta
Spinach Lasagna Twirls
Three-Cheese Manicotti

Desserts
Peach Dream
Ricotta Cake Italiana
Mixed Fruit and Nut Cookies
Blueberry Angel Food Cake

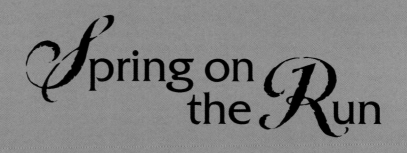

Spring on the Run

weeknight and busy weekend recipes

Banana, Peanut Butter and Chocolate Smoothie

Serves 1

1 ripe banana, sliced
2 cups ice cubes
3/4 cup milk
1/4 cup vanilla yogurt
1/4 cup chocolate sauce
1/4 cup chunky peanut butter

*C*ombine the banana, ice, milk, yogurt, chocolate sauce and peanut butter in a blender and process until smooth. Pour into a glass and serve immediately.

Tropical Blend Smoothie

Add one and one-half ounces of rum per serving to turn this smoothie into a tropical cocktail.

Serves 2

1 very ripe banana, sliced
1 cup chopped fresh mango
1 cup chopped fresh pineapple
1 cup unsweetened pineapple juice
1/2 cup light or regular unsweetened coconut milk
1 teaspoon fresh lime juice

*A*rrange the banana, mango and pineapple in a single layer on a sheet pan and freeze, covered, for 2 hours or until firm. Combine the frozen fruit, pineapple juice, coconut milk and lime juice in a blender and process until thick and smooth. Pour into glasses and serve immediately. For a thinner consistency, add additional pineapple juice.

Very Berry Smoothie

Serves 2

1³/₄ cups reduced-fat blueberry yogurt
¹/₄ cup grape juice
1¹/₂ cups frozen blueberries

1 cup frozen blackberries
1 cup skim milk
1 cup ice cubes

*C*ombine the yogurt and grape juice in a blender. Add the blueberries, blackberries, skim milk and ice cubes and process until thick and smooth. Pour into glasses and serve immediately.

Fish Stew à la Provençal

Serves 4 to 6

1 large onion, chopped
¹/₂ cup chopped celery with leaves
1 large garlic clove, crushed
2 tablespoons butter
2 (16-ounce) cans diced tomatoes
¹/₂ cup dry white wine
¹/₂ cup minced fresh parsley
1 teaspoon salt
¹/₄ teaspoon pepper
¹/₄ teaspoon thyme
1 pound fish fillets, cut into 1-inch pieces

*S*auté the onion, celery and garlic in the butter in a large saucepan until the onion and celery are tender. Add the undrained tomatoes, wine, parsley, salt, pepper and thyme and mix well.

Simmer, covered, for 30 minutes, stirring occasionally. Add the fish and simmer for 7 to 10 minutes longer, stirring occasionally. Ladle into soup bowls and serve with a green salad and crusty French bread. For variety, substitute frozen shrimp for the fish. Add the shrimp to the soup mixture and bring to a boil. Remove from the heat and let stand for 1 minute before serving.

Crab Chowder

Serves 6 to 8

4 potatoes, peeled and chopped
1 yellow onion, chopped
2 ribs celery, chopped
1/2 cup (1 stick) butter
3/4 cup flour
10 slices bacon, partially cooked and chopped
1 (16-ounce) can corn, drained
1/4 cup chopped fresh parsley
1 teaspoon seafood seasoning
1/4 teaspoon paprika
1/4 teaspoon garlic salt
1/4 teaspoon celery salt
1/4 teaspoon white pepper
Salt and freshly ground black pepper to taste
4 cups milk
1 pound crab meat, drained and shells removed
2 cups heavy cream

*P*arboil the potatoes in boiling water in a saucepan for 5 minutes; drain. Sauté the onion and celery in the butter in a stockpot over medium heat for 2 minutes or until tender. Reduce the heat to low and stir in the flour. Cook for 2 to 3 minutes or until bubbly, stirring constantly. Add the potatoes, bacon, corn, parsley, seafood seasoning, paprika, garlic salt, celery salt, white pepper, salt and black pepper and mix gently. Add the milk gradually, stirring constantly.

Bring to a boil and boil for 20 to 30 minutes, stirring occasionally. Fold in the crab meat and reduce the heat to a simmer. Stir in the heavy cream and simmer just until heated through, stirring frequently; do not boil. Taste and adjust the seasonings and ladle into soup bowls. For a thinner consistency, add additional milk, vegetable broth or fish stock. You may substitute imitation crab meat for the fresh crab meat.

Spring Minestrone

Serves 8

1 onion, chopped
1/3 cup olive oil
1 large carrot, cut into
   1/2-inch slices
1 rib celery, cut into
   1/2-inch slices
3 garlic cloves,
   finely chopped
41/2 cups reduced-sodium
   chicken broth
1 (28-ounce) can
   whole tomatoes
1 (15-ounce) can white
   beans, drained
2 zucchini, cut into
   1/2-inch slices
4 ounces fresh green beans,
   trimmed and cut into
   1/2-inch pieces

4 ounces fresh broccoli,
   cut into 1/2-inch pieces
4 cups shredded
   green cabbage
1 cup frozen green peas
1 tablespoon oregano
1 bay leaf
2 teaspoons crushed
   red pepper
Salt and black pepper
   to taste
2 cups cooked
   elbow macaroni
Freshly grated Parmesan
   cheese to taste
Olive oil to taste
Garlic bruschetta
Dry-cured sausages

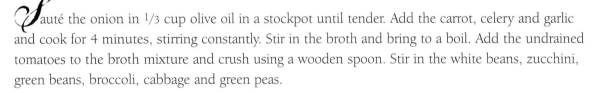

A mainstay in the Valley for sixty-seven years, The Junior League of Phoenix Rummage Sale is considered "Arizona's Largest Garage Sale." Every February, more than 5,000 people wait anxiously in the parking lot at the Arizona State Fairgrounds for an opportunity to find the many treasures that abound. This one-day secondhand sale features everything from clothing to furniture, jewelry to antiques and collectibles, household items to baby gear. It is a complete treasure trove of slightly used items from our own League members' homes. The Rummage Sale provides quality merchandise at an extremely affordable price to thousands of people each year. It also provides important financial resources to the community programs that The Junior League of Phoenix supports, raising more than $100,000 per year.

Sauté the onion in 1/3 cup olive oil in a stockpot until tender. Add the carrot, celery and garlic and cook for 4 minutes, stirring constantly. Stir in the broth and bring to a boil. Add the undrained tomatoes to the broth mixture and crush using a wooden spoon. Stir in the white beans, zucchini, green beans, broccoli, cabbage and green peas.

Bring to a boil over high heat and add the oregano, bay leaf and red pepper; reduce the heat. Simmer for 1 hour or until the cabbage wilts and the vegetables are tender, stirring occasionally. Discard the bay leaf and season with salt and black pepper.

To serve, spoon 1/4 cup of the pasta into each of 8 soup bowls and ladle the soup over the pasta. Sprinkle each serving with Parmesan cheese and drizzle with olive oil to taste. Serve with bruschetta and sausages.

Black-Eyed Pea and Hominy Salad

Serves 6 to 8

2 (15-ounce) cans black-eyed peas, drained
1 (15-ounce) can yellow hominy or
    corn, drained
3 tomatoes, chopped
1 small yellow onion, chopped

1 cup chopped fresh cilantro
Chopped tops of 5 green onions
3 garlic cloves, minced
1/2 (16-ounce) bottle classic vinaigrette
Salt and pepper to taste

*C*ombine the black-eyed peas, hominy, tomatoes, onion, cilantro, green onion tops and garlic in a salad bowl and mix gently. Add the vinaigrette and toss to coat. Season with salt and pepper. Chill, covered, for 8 to 10 hours.

Strawberry Spinach Salad

Serves 4 to 6

Poppy Seed Dressing
1 cup olive oil
1/2 cup sugar
1/4 cup white vinegar
1/4 cup raspberry vinegar
1 tablespoon poppy seeds
1 teaspoon salt
1 teaspoon dry mustard

Salad
10 to 16 ounces fresh spinach, trimmed
8 ounces fresh strawberries, sliced
1/2 cup chopped pecans

*F*or the dressing, combine the olive oil, sugar, white vinegar, raspberry vinegar, poppy seeds, salt and dry mustard in a blender and process until incorporated.

For the salad, toss the spinach, strawberries and pecans in a salad bowl. Add the desired amount of dressing and toss to coat. Serve immediately.

Tortellini Salad

Serves 8

Green Onion Vinaigrette

1/2 cup sliced green onions
1/3 cup red wine vinegar
1/3 cup vegetable oil
1/3 cup olive oil
2 tablespoons chopped fresh parsley
2 garlic cloves, minced
2 teaspoons basil
1 1/2 teaspoons Dijon mustard
1 teaspoon dill weed
1 teaspoon salt
1/2 teaspoon pepper

1/2 teaspoon sugar
1/2 teaspoon oregano

Salad

2 cups fresh snow peas
2 cups broccoli florets
8 ounces cheese tortellini
2 1/2 cups cherry tomato halves
2 cups sliced fresh mushrooms
1 (7-ounce) can pitted whole black
   olives, drained
3 tablespoons grated Parmesan cheese

*F*or the vinaigrette, combine the green onions, vinegar, vegetable oil, olive oil, parsley, garlic, basil, mustard, dill weed, salt, pepper, sugar and oregano in a jar with a tight-fitting lid and seal tightly. Shake to mix.

For the salad, blanch the snow peas and broccoli in boiling water in a saucepan for 1 minute. Plunge the vegetables into a bowl of ice water to stop the cooking process and drain. Cook the pasta using the package directions; drain.

Combine the pasta, snow peas, broccoli, tomatoes, mushrooms, olives and Parmesan cheese in a bowl and mix gently. Add the vinaigrette and toss to coat. Chill, covered, for several hours. For variety, add 1 pound deveined peeled cooked shrimp.

Pacific Rim Seafood Salad

Perfect for a luncheon. For a festive presentation, spoon the salad in the shape of a wreath onto a silver tray and fill the center with fresh parsley.

Serves 4

Curry Chutney Dressing

1 cup mayonnaise

1/2 cup sour cream

2 tablespoons mango chutney

1 teaspoon curry powder

Salad

8 ounces deveined peeled cooked shrimp

8 ounces crab meat, drained and
   shells removed

1 cup chopped celery

1 (8-ounce) can water chestnuts, drained

1/2 cup chopped green onions (white and
   green parts)

2 tablespoons golden raisins

Fresh or drained canned sweetened
   pineapple chunks

*F*or the dressing, combine the mayonnaise, sour cream, chutney and curry powder in a bowl and mix well.

For the salad, mix the shrimp, crab meat, celery, water chestnuts, green onions and raisins in a bowl. Add the dressing to the shrimp mixture and toss to coat. Chill, covered, in the refrigerator. Stir in the pineapple chunks just before serving.

Glazed Carrots

Serves 4

1 tablespoon unsalted butter

3 or 4 carrots, peeled and roll cut

1/4 cup white wine

1/2 teaspoon sugar

Salt and pepper to taste

*M*elt the butter in a sauté pan over medium heat. Sauté the carrots in the butter for 3 to 4 minutes; do not brown. Add the wine and cook for 3 to 4 minutes or until the liquid is reduced, stirring frequently. Add the sugar, salt and pepper and cook until the sugar dissolves. Serve immediately. To roll cut carrots, place 1 peeled carrot on a hard surface. Make a diagonal cut to remove the stem end. Hold the knife in the same position and roll the carrot 180 degrees, a half turn. Slice through it on the same diagonal, forming a piece with 2 angled edges. Repeat with the remaining carrots.

Portobello and Mushroom Brie Cups

Makes 2 dozen cups

6 ounces portobello or cremini mushrooms, finely chopped
2 garlic cloves, minced
1 large shallot, minced
2 tablespoons unsalted butter
1/4 cup chopped green onions (white and green parts)
1 teaspoon Dijon mustard
1/4 cup bread crumbs
3 tablespoons grated Parmesan cheese
1 tablespoon minced flat-leaf parsley
1 teaspoon balsamic vinegar
1 (8-count) can crescent rolls
3 ounces Brie cheese, cut into 24 pieces

*P*reheat the oven to 375 degrees. Spray 24 miniature muffin cups with nonstick cooking spray. Sauté the mushrooms, garlic and shallot in the butter in a skillet for 5 to 6 minutes or until the mushrooms are tender. Stir in the green onions and mustard. Remove from the heat and mix in the bread crumbs, Parmesan cheese, parsley and vinegar.

Unroll the roll dough into 4 rectangles and press the perforations to seal. Cut each rectangle into 6 squares. Press 1 dough square over the bottom and up the sides of each prepared muffin cup, allowing the corners to stand above the tops of the muffin cups. Spoon 1 to 2 tablespoons of the mushroom mixture into each muffin cup. Bake for 10 to 12 minutes or until golden brown. Top each with 1 piece of the Brie and bake for 2 to 4 minutes longer or until the cheese melts. Cool slightly before serving.

The mushroom filling may be prepared up to 12 hours in advance and stored, covered, in the refrigerator. The cups may be prepared in advance and baked at 375 degrees for 10 minutes or until light brown. Store in an airtight container at room temperature. Just before serving, spoon the filling into the baked cups and top with the Brie. Bake at 375 degrees for 4 to 6 minutes or until the cheese melts and the filling is heated through.

Crisp Rosemary Roasted Potatoes

Serves 4

2 pounds red potatoes, cut into 1/4-inch slices
1 tablespoon olive oil
2 tablespoons chopped fresh rosemary
Salt and pepper to taste

Preheat the oven to 450 degrees. Arrange the potatoes in a single layer on 2 greased baking sheets. Brush the potatoes with the olive oil and sprinkle with the rosemary, salt and pepper.

Place the baking sheets on the oven racks in the upper and lower thirds of the oven. Roast for 25 to 30 minutes or until brown and crisp, switching the positions of the baking sheets halfway through the roasting process.

Cheddar Cheese Biscuits

Makes 2 dozen biscuits

4 cups unbleached flour
2 tablespoons plus 2 teaspoons baking powder
2 teaspoons sugar
1 teaspoon salt
1 cup (2 sticks) unsalted butter, chilled and cut into 1/2-inch cubes
13/4 cups heavy cream, chilled
2 cups (8 ounces) shredded sharp Cheddar cheese

Preheat the oven to 425 degrees. Combine the flour, baking powder, sugar and salt in a food processor and process until blended. Add the butter and pulse until crumbly. Add 11/2 cups of the heavy cream and process until the dough adheres, adding the remaining heavy cream as needed for the desired consistency.

Combine the dough and cheese in a bowl and mix well. Knead on a lightly floured surface for 30 seconds. Pat the dough 1 inch thick and cut into rounds with a 2-inch cutter. Arrange the rounds on an ungreased baking sheet and bake for 15 minutes. Serve immediately.

Sesame Ginger Beef Stir-Fry

Fish sauce may be purchased from Asian markets and in the Asian food section of many supermarkets.

Serves 4

1 pound lean top sirloin, cut into thin strips
3 tablespoons soy sauce
2/3 cup beef broth
1 tablespoon fish sauce (nam pla)
1 tablespoon dry sherry
2 teaspoons cornstarch
1 teaspoon sugar
1/4 cup peanut oil or vegetable oil
1 teaspoon Oriental sesame oil
1 small bunch green onions, cut diagonally into 11/2-inch pieces
1 pound thin asparagus, trimmed and cut diagonally into 11/2-inch pieces
1 small red bell pepper, cut into 1/4-inch pieces
2 garlic cloves, minced
11/2 tablespoons minced fresh gingerroot
2 teaspoons sesame seeds

Combine the beef and soy sauce in a resealable plastic bag and seal tightly. Turn to coat. Marinate in the refrigerator for 1 to 10 hours, turning occasionally. Whisk the broth, fish sauce, sherry, cornstarch and sugar in a measuring cup until blended.

Heat 2 tablespoons of the peanut oil in a large skillet over high heat. Add the beef in batches in a single layer to the hot skillet. Cook undisturbed for 11/2 minutes or until the beef begins to blacken on the bottom; turn. Cook for 1 minute longer or until brown on the remaining side. Remove the beef to a plate using a slotted spoon, reserving the pan drippings.

Heat the remaining 2 tablespoons peanut oil and sesame oil with the reserved pan drippings over medium-high heat. Reserve 1/2 cup of the green onions. Add the remaining green onions, asparagus, bell pepper, garlic and gingerroot to the peanut oil mixture. Stir-fry for 2 minutes or until the vegetables are slightly brown and tender-crisp. Add the broth mixture and bring to a boil. Return the beef to the skillet.

Cook for 3 minutes or until the sauce thickens, stirring frequently. Spoon the beef mixture onto a serving platter and sprinkle with the reserved green onions and sesame seeds. Serve with jasmine rice and a cucumber, red bell pepper and sweet onion salad dressed with rice wine dressing.

Curried Meatballs

Serves 6

1 pound ground beef
2 eggs, beaten
1/4 cup unseasoned bread crumbs
1/4 cup chopped onion
2 garlic cloves, minced
1 tablespoon parsley flakes
3/4 teaspoon salt
3/4 teaspoon curry powder
1/4 teaspoon pepper
1/2 large onion, sliced

1 tablespoon vegetable oil
1 (14-ounce) can coconut milk
1 (14-ounce) can chicken broth
3/4 teaspoon curry powder
1/2 cup raisins
1 (8-ounce) package frozen peas
1/2 cup almonds, toasted
3 cups instant rice
1/2 cup shredded coconut, toasted
1/4 cup chopped green onions

*C*ombine the ground beef, eggs, bread crumbs, chopped onion, garlic, parsley flakes, salt, 3/4 teaspoon curry powder and pepper in a bowl and mix well. Shape the ground beef mixture by rounded tablespoonfuls into 18 meatballs.

Sauté the sliced onion in the oil in a large skillet for 5 minutes. Add the coconut milk, broth and 3/4 teaspoon curry powder and bring to a boil, stirring occasionally. Add the meatballs and raisins and mix gently; reduce the heat.

Simmer, covered, for 15 minutes, turning the meatballs halfway through the cooking process. Stir in the peas and almonds and return to a boil. Add the rice and mix well. Remove from the heat. Let stand, covered, for 5 minutes. Spoon into a serving bowl and sprinkle with the coconut and green onions.

Spring Leg of Lamb with Tomato and Herb Vinaigrette

Serves 10

Lamb

1/4 cup chopped fresh mint
1/4 cup chopped fresh basil
1/4 cup chopped green onions
2 tablespoons chopped fresh marjoram
2 tablespoons balsamic vinegar
1 tablespoon olive oil
Salt and pepper to taste
1 (6- to 7-pound) leg of lamb

Tomato and Herb Vinaigrette

1 1/4 cups olive oil
3/4 cup chopped fresh mint
2/3 cup chopped fresh basil
10 tablespoons red wine vinegar
2 1/2 tablespoons chopped fresh marjoram
2 1/2 tablespoons whole-grain Dijon mustard
1 1/4 teaspoons sugar
1 1/4 teaspoons salt
1 2/3 cups chopped seeded fresh plum tomatoes
Pepper to taste

*F*or the lamb, combine the mint, basil, green onions, marjoram, vinegar and olive oil in a bowl and mix well. Season with salt and pepper. Arrange the lamb in a large baking dish and rub the mint mixture over the surface of the lamb. Chill, covered, for 8 to 10 hours.

Preheat the oven to 450 degrees. Place the lamb in a large roasting pan and roast for 20 minutes. Reduce the heat to 350 degrees and roast for 1 1/4 hours longer or until a meat thermometer inserted in the thickest portion of the lamb registers 145 degrees for medium-rare. Tent with foil and let stand for 20 minutes before slicing.

For the vinaigrette, whisk the olive oil, mint, basil, vinegar, marjoram, mustard, sugar and salt in a bowl until incorporated. Stir in the tomatoes and season with pepper. Serve with the lamb.

Chicken Oporto

Even when preparing a sit-down meal, pick recipes such as this that can be prepared in advance of your guests' arrival and reheated just before serving. You want to enjoy your guests and not be stuck in the kitchen.

Serves 4

1/2 cup (1 stick) butter
8 ounces fresh mushrooms, thinly sliced
1/4 cup flour
2 teaspoons salt
1/4 teaspoon pepper
1/4 teaspoon nutmeg
8 boneless skinless chicken breasts
11/2 cups heavy cream
1/3 cup white port

Heat the butter in a 12-inch skillet over medium-high heat. Add the mushrooms to the skillet and cook for 5 minutes, stirring frequently. Remove the mushrooms to a bowl using a slotted spoon, reserving the pan juices.

Mix the flour, salt, pepper and nutmeg on a sheet of waxed paper. Coat the chicken with the flour mixture and sauté in the reserved pan juices until brown on both sides. Stir in the mushrooms, heavy cream and wine. Reduce the heat to low and simmer, covered, for 15 minutes or until the chicken is cooked through, stirring occasionally. Serve over hot cooked egg noodles if desired.

Chicken Pesto Pan Pizza

Serves 6 to 8 as an entrée, or 24 as an appetizer

1 can refrigerator pizza dough
1 (10-ounce) package frozen chopped spinach,
   thawed and drained
1 (8-ounce) jar pesto
1/2 cup ricotta cheese
1/4 cup chopped onion

2 cups shredded cooked chicken
Sliced fresh mushrooms
Sliced plum tomatoes
1 cup (4 ounces) shredded Swiss cheese
1/4 cup (1 ounce) grated Romano cheese

Preheat the oven to 425 degrees. Unroll the pizza dough and pat into a rectangle on a 10×15-inch baking sheet, building up the edges slightly to form a rim. Pierce with a fork. Bake for 7 minutes or until light brown. Maintain the oven temperature.

Press the excess moisture from the spinach. Combine the spinach, pesto, ricotta cheese and onion in a bowl and mix well. Spread the spinach mixture over the baked layer and top with the chicken, mushrooms, tomatoes, Swiss cheese and Romano cheese. Bake for 7 minutes or until the cheese melts and the crust is golden brown.

Baked Fish Italienne

Serves 4

1/4 cup (1/2 stick) butter
2 1/2 to 3 pounds trout or red snapper fillets
1/4 cup lemon juice

1/4 cup Worcestershire sauce
Seasoned bread crumbs to taste

Preheat the oven to 450 degrees. Lightly brown the butter in a large baking dish in the oven. Coat the fillets with the browned butter and arrange skin side down in the heated baking dish. Mix the lemon juice and Worcestershire sauce in a bowl and drizzle over the fillets.

Bake for 15 minutes or until the fillets flake easily, basting once or twice with the pan juices. Remove from the oven and sprinkle the fillets with bread crumbs. Baste again with the pan juices and bake for 5 minutes longer. Serve immediately.

Gnocchi with Chicken, Sun-Dried Tomatoes, Gorgonzola and Pine Nuts

Serves 4

16 ounces gnocchi
Salt to taste
2 tablespoons sun-dried tomato oil
2 boneless skinless chicken breasts (9 ounces)
4 garlic cloves, minced
1/2 cup chopped drained oil-pack sun-dried tomatoes
1/2 cup chopped fresh basil
1/2 cup canned reduced-sodium chicken broth
1/2 cup (2 ounces) crumbled Gorgonzola cheese
1/4 cup chopped prosciutto
Pepper to taste
1/4 cup pine nuts, toasted

Cook the gnocchi in boiling salted water in a saucepan just until al dente. Drain and cover to keep warm. Heat 1 tablespoon of the sun-dried tomato oil in a large heavy skillet over medium-high heat. Sauté the chicken in the hot oil for 5 to 8 minutes per side or until cooked through. Remove the chicken to a plate using a slotted spoon, reserving the pan drippings. Chop the chicken into 1/2-inch pieces.

Heat the remaining 1 tablespoon sun-dried tomato oil with the reserved pan drippings over medium-high heat. Sauté the garlic in the hot oil for 1 minute. Stir in the chicken, sun-dried tomatoes, basil, broth, cheese and prosciutto and bring to a boil, stirring occasionally. Toss the chicken mixture with the gnocchi in a bowl. Season with salt and pepper, sprinkle with the pine nuts and serve immediately.

Seafood Pasta

Serves 4

12 ounces pasta

2 tablespoons butter

1 tablespoon vegetable oil

1 cup chopped onion

1 cup dry white wine

1 tablespoon chicken bouillon granules

1 teaspoon basil

1/8 teaspoon pepper

12 ounces deveined peeled shrimp or scallops

6 to 8 plum tomatoes, peeled, seeded
   and chopped

3 tablespoons butter, melted

1/2 cup (2 ounces) grated Parmesan cheese

1/2 cup snipped fresh parsley

Cook the pasta using the package directions. Drain and cover to keep warm. Heat 2 tablespoons butter and the oil in a skillet. Cook the onion in the butter mixture until tender, stirring frequently. Stir in the wine, bouillon granules, basil and pepper and bring to a boil; reduce the heat. Cook until the liquid is reduced by 1/2, stirring occasionally. Add the shrimp and tomatoes and mix well. Increase the heat and cook for 5 minutes or until the shrimp turn pink, stirring frequently. Toss the pasta with 3 tablespoons melted butter in a serving bowl. Add the shrimp sauce and mix well. Sprinkle with the cheese and parsley and serve immediately.

Spinach Lasagna Twirls

Serves 4

1 (10-ounce) package frozen chopped spinach,
   thawed and drained

15 ounces ricotta cheese

1/2 cup (2 ounces) grated Parmesan cheese

1/4 cup chopped fresh basil

1/4 teaspoon nutmeg

Salt and pepper to taste

1 (26- to 30-ounce) jar spaghetti sauce

12 lasagna noodles, cooked and drained

2 cups (8 ounces) shredded mozzarella cheese

Chopped fresh flat-leaf parsley

Preheat the oven to 350 degrees. Press the excess moisture from the spinach. Combine the spinach, ricotta cheese, Parmesan cheese, basil, nutmeg, salt and pepper in a bowl and mix well. Spread a thin layer of the spaghetti sauce over the bottom of an ungreased 9×13-inch baking pan. Spread 1/4 cup of the spinach mixture over 1 side of each noodle and roll to enclose the filling. Cut diagonally into halves and arrange cut side down in the prepared pan. Spoon the remaining sauce over the stuffed noodles and sprinkle with the mozzarella cheese. Bake, covered, for 25 minutes or until bubbly. Sprinkle with parsley. Serve in pasta bowls and garnish with sprigs of fresh basil if desired.

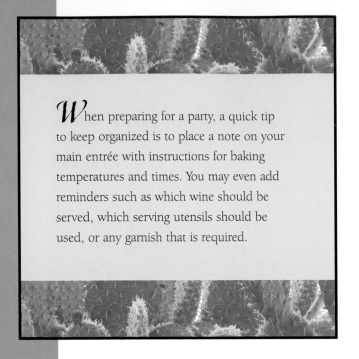

Three-Cheese Manicotti

Serves 6

1 cup small curd cottage cheese
1 cup (4 ounces) grated Romano cheese
1 cup (4 ounces) shredded Muenster cheese
1/2 cup black olives, chopped
2 eggs, lightly beaten
1/2 teaspoon oregano
1/4 teaspoon salt
1/8 teaspoon pepper
12 manicotti shells
1 (14-ounce) can tomato or spaghetti sauce
1/2 cup (2 ounces) shredded Romano cheese
1/4 cup black olives, sliced

Combine the cottage cheese, 1 cup Romano cheese, Muenster cheese, chopped olives, eggs, oregano, salt and pepper in a bowl and mix well.

Add 4 of the pasta shells to a large saucepan of boiling water and boil for 5 to 7 minutes or until al dente. Remove to a colander with a slotted spoon to drain. Repeat the process with the remaining pasta shells.

Preheat the oven to 350 degrees. Spread 1 cup of the sauce in a greased baking dish. Stuff the pasta shells with the cottage cheese mixture and arrange in a single layer in the prepared baking dish. Pour the remaining sauce over the shells and sprinkle with 1/2 cup Romano cheese and the sliced olives. Bake for 25 to 30 minutes or until bubbly.

Peach Dream

Serves 6 to 8

3 egg whites
1/2 teaspoon cream of tartar
1 cup sugar
3/4 to 1 cup saltine cracker crumbs
    (about 14 to 18 crackers)

1 cup chopped nuts (optional)
1 teaspoon vanilla extract
2 to 4 large peaches, peeled and sliced
Whipped cream

*P*reheat the oven to 350 degrees. Beat the egg whites in a mixing bowl until foamy. Add the cream of tartar and beat until stiff peaks form. Fold in the sugar, cracker crumbs, nuts and vanilla. Spread the egg white mixture in a buttered 9- or 10-inch baking dish or 8×8-inch baking pan. Bake for 10 to 15 minutes or until light brown. Let stand until cool. You may prepare to this point up to 1 day in advance and store at room temperature.

Arrange the sliced peaches over the top of the baked layer and spread with whipped cream. Chill until serving time. You may substitute sliced strawberries, blueberries or drained thawed frozen peaches for the fresh peaches.

Ricotta Cake Italiana

Serves 15

2 pounds ricotta cheese
4 eggs
3/4 cup sugar

2 teaspoons vanilla or anisette extract
1 (2-layer) package yellow cake mix
Confectioners' sugar to taste

*P*reheat the oven to 350 degrees. Combine the ricotta cheese, eggs, sugar and vanilla in a mixing bowl and beat until smooth, scraping the bowl occasionally. Prepare the cake mix using the package directions and spread in a greased 9×13-inch cake pan. Spread the ricotta cheese mixture over the top of the prepared layer.

Bake for 45 to 55 minutes or until the edges pull away from the sides of the pan. Cool in the pan on a wire rack and dust lightly with confectioners' sugar. Serve with fresh berries.

Mixed Fruit and Nut Cookies

Makes 3 dozen cookies

2 1/4 cups flour
1 teaspoon baking soda
1 teaspoon salt
1 cup (1/2 stick) unsalted butter, softened
1 cup packed brown sugar
1/2 cup sugar
2 eggs
1 teaspoon vanilla extract
1 1/2 cups (9 ounces) white chocolate chips
1 1/2 cups shredded coconut
1 1/2 cups chopped dried apricots
1 1/2 cups dried cherries
1 1/2 cups blanched almonds
1/2 cup chopped pistachios

*P*reheat the oven to 375 degrees. Line a cookie sheet with baking parchment. Mix the flour, baking soda and salt together. Beat the butter, brown sugar and sugar in a mixing bowl for 3 minutes or until light and fluffy, scraping the bowl occasionally. Add the eggs 1 at a time, beating well after each addition. Beat in the vanilla until blended. Add the flour mixture all at once and beat at low speed just until combined. Beat in the chocolate chips, coconut, apricots, cherries, almonds and pistachios.

Drop the dough by spoonfuls 2 inches apart onto the prepared cookie sheet. Bake for 12 to 15 minutes or until golden brown. Cool on baking parchment on a wire rack. Store in an airtight container.

Blueberry Angel Food Cake

Serves 8

Cake

1 cup sifted cake flour

1/2 cup sugar

12 egg whites

11/4 teaspoons cream of tartar

1/2 teaspoon salt

1 cup sugar

11/2 cups fresh or frozen blueberries

1 teaspoon vanilla extract

2 tablespoons sifted cake flour

1 tablespoon grated lemon zest

Lemon Glaze and Assembly

2 cups confectioners' sugar

1/2 cup fresh lemon juice

Finely grated zest of 1 lemon

1 tablespoon unsalted butter

Splash of limoncello (optional)

Whipped cream

Fresh blueberries

Fresh mint leaves

*F*or the cake, preheat the oven to 375 degrees. Sift 1 cup cake flour and 1/2 cup sugar into a bowl and mix well. Beat the egg whites in a mixing bowl at high speed until foamy. Add the cream of tartar and salt and beat until soft peaks form. Add 1 cup sugar 2 tablespoons at a time, beating constantly until stiff peaks form. Sift the cake flour mixture 1/4 cup at a time over the egg white mixture and fold in. Fold in the blueberries and vanilla.

Mix 2 tablespoons cake flour and the lemon zest in a bowl. Sprinkle over the egg white mixture and fold in. Spoon the batter into an ungreased 10-inch tube pan. Bake for 40 minutes or until the cake springs back when lightly touched. Invert the pan onto a wire rack and let stand until cool.

For the glaze, mix the confectioners' sugar and lemon juice in a microwave-safe bowl and stir until the sugar dissolves. Add the lemon zest, butter and liqueur and microwave for 30 seconds. Whisk until smooth.

To assemble, loosen the cake from the side of the pan with a sharp knife and remove the pan. Drizzle with the glaze and garnish each serving with whipped cream, fresh blueberries and fresh mint.

With nearly 350 days of sun each year, Phoenicians enjoy participating in outdoor activities year-round, whether it's a casual walk in the park, a swim in the pool, or an extreme adventure sport. Camelback Mountain sits in the center of the Valley, attracting rock climbers and hikers, while the park at Tempe Town Lake is seen filled with families picnicking and enjoying the many water activities. Phoenix is home to more than two hundred prestigious golf courses, where golfers come to test their game on signature courses designed by professionals such as Arnold Palmer and Jack Nicklaus. After a day of physical activity, replenish your body and soul with a nourishing meal.

It's a Dry Heat

photo donated by 3rios fototeca
photo © Adalberto R. Lanz

Cocktails
Arizona Sunrise
Melon Cooler
Sea Breeze
Caipirinha

Appetizers
Nutty Grape Clusters
Sun-Dried Tomato Dip
Blue Cheese Puffs
Asian Turkey Lettuce Wraps

Salads
Sensation Salad
Hot Grain Salad
Chicken, Cantaloupe and Dill Salad
Barbecued Chicken and Grape Salad

Main Courses
Flank Steak with Arugula Salad
Tarragon Chicken Breasts
Miso-Glazed Fillet of Fish
Salmon in Orange and White Wine Marinade
Seared Scallops with Lime Chile Sauce
Orzo Risotto with Peas, Prosciutto and Onion
Tortellini with Spinach Walnut Pesto

Desserts
Creamy Fruit Delight
Kahlúa Brandy Freeze
Dulce de Leche and Strawberry Ice Cream Cake
Coconut Lemon Bars
Summer Fruit Crisp

It's a Dry Heat

lite and casual summer dishes

Arizona Sunrise

Serves 1

Cracked ice
4 ounces orange juice
2 ounces tequila
Lime juice to taste
1 teaspoon grenadine
1 lime slice

*F*ill a 12-ounce glass halfway with cracked ice. Pour the orange juice, tequila and lime juice over the ice and stir. Drizzle with the grenadine; do not stir. Garnish with the lime slice and serve immediately.

Melon Cooler

Serves 2

2 cups crushed ice
6 (1-ounce) chunks cantaloupe
3 ounces rum
1 ounce orange liqueur
1 ounce fresh lemon juice
1 teaspoon sugar
Fresh mint leaves

*C*ombine the ice, cantaloupe, rum, liqueur, lemon juice and sugar in a blender and process until smooth. Pour into small hurricane glasses and garnish with mint leaves.

Sea Breeze

Serves 1

Ice cubes
2 ounces vodka
2 ounces cranberry juice
2 ounces fresh grapefruit juice
1 lime wedge

*F*ill a highball glass with ice. Pour the vodka, cranberry juice and grapefruit juice over the ice and stir gently. Squeeze the juice from the lime wedge into the drink and then add the lime wedge. Serve immediately.

Caipirinha

Brazil's national drink.

Serves 1

1/2 lime, coarsely chopped
1 teaspoon superfine sugar
1 cup (or more) cracked ice
1 1/2 ounces cachaça
1 lime slice

*P*lace the chopped lime in a cocktail shaker and sprinkle with the sugar. Crush the lime with a pestle or spoon, working for 1 to 2 minutes to release the oils from the peel. Add the cracked ice and brandy and shake vigorously for 30 seconds. Pour into an old-fashioned glass and garnish with the lime slice.

*T*ourism has provided our state with the nickname of the "Valley of the Sun" due to the mountains that surround the greater Phoenix area and nearly 350 days per year of sun. Visitors come from all over the country to enjoy this magnificent environment. Many a tourist has come for a visit, fallen in love with our weather and landscape, and before they know it, they are calling Arizona home.

Nutty Grape Clusters

Serves 3 to 4

5 ounces garlic and fine herb-flavor cheese
spread or boursin, softened
18 red or green seedless grapes
(about 1 pound)

1/2 cup pistachios, finely chopped
1/2 cup hazelnuts, finely chopped
Grape leaves (optional)

*S*hape about 1 teaspoon of the cheese spread around each grape and roll between palms to form a ball. Chill for 30 minutes or until firm. Roll 9 of the grapes in the chopped pistachios and the remaining 9 grapes in the chopped hazelnuts.

Arrange the grapes on a platter in the shape of a grape cluster and garnish with grape leaves if desired.

Sun-Dried Tomato Dip

Makes 2 cups

8 ounces cream cheese, softened
1/2 cup sour cream
1/2 cup mayonnaise
1/4 cup drained oil-pack sun-dried
tomatoes, chopped

10 dashes Tabasco sauce, or to taste
1 teaspoon salt
1 teaspoon pepper
1 green onion, sliced (white and green parts)

*C*ombine the cream cheese, sour cream, mayonnaise, sun-dried tomatoes, Tabasco sauce, salt and pepper in a food processor and process until puréed. Add the green onion and pulse twice. Chill, covered, until serving time.

Bring the sun-dried tomato mixture to room temperature and serve with baguette slices, melba toast rounds, broccoli florets, sugar snap peas and/or orange and yellow bell pepper strips.

Blue Cheese Puffs

Makes 5 dozen puffs

16 ounces cream cheese, softened
1 cup mayonnaise
3/4 to 1 cup (3 to 4 ounces) crumbled blue cheese
1/4 cup minced fresh chives
1 tablespoon minced onion
1/4 to 1/2 teaspoon cayenne pepper, or to taste
1 loaf freshly baked whole wheat bread, thinly sliced
Paprika to taste

*C*ombine the cream cheese and mayonnaise in a bowl
and mix well. Stir in the blue cheese, chives, onion and
cayenne pepper.

Cut 1 1/2- to 2-inch rounds from the bread slices using
a round cutter. Spread 1 tablespoon of the cream cheese
mixture on each round and arrange in a single layer on
a baking sheet. Freeze until firm.

Preheat the oven to 350 degrees. Bake for 15 minutes or
until the puffs are light brown. Sprinkle with paprika and
serve immediately. You may store in an airtight container.

*S*tock your pantry with the following staples
and you will be able to prepare a quick and
nutritious meal on a minute's notice:

• Canned beans
• Canned tuna
• Canned roasted bell peppers
• Canned artichoke hearts
• Canned sun-dried tomatoes
• Chicken, beef, or vegetable broth
• Variety of pastas
• Bread crumbs
• Tomato sauce
• Tomato paste
• Canned tomatoes
• Olives
• Rice
• Dried fruits

Asian Turkey Lettuce Wraps

Makes 1 dozen wraps

1 tablespoon peanut oil
1 large onion, chopped
2 garlic cloves, minced
1 1/4 pounds lean ground turkey
1/2 cup Asian peanut sauce
1 tablespoon hoisin sauce
1 tablespoon soy sauce
Juice of 1/2 lime
1 teaspoon chopped jalapeño chile
1 cucumber, peeled, seeded and chopped (about 1 1/4 cups)
1/4 cup coarsely chopped fresh mint
1/4 cup chopped fresh cilantro
Salt and pepper to taste
12 large butter or iceberg lettuce leaves
1/4 cup salted peanuts, chopped
Soy sauce for dipping

Heat the peanut oil in a large heavy skillet over medium-high heat. Sauté the onion and garlic in the hot oil for 3 minutes or until the onion begins to brown. Add the turkey and sauté for 7 minutes or until brown and crumbly; drain. Stir in the peanut sauce, hoisin sauce, 1 tablespoon soy sauce, lime juice and jalapeño chile.

Cook just until heated through, stirring frequently. You may prepare to this point up to 8 hours in advance and store, covered, in the refrigerator. Reheat in the microwave or skillet, adding water as needed for the desired consistency. Stir in the cucumber, mint, cilantro, salt and pepper. Spoon the turkey mixture into a bowl.

To serve, spoon some of the turkey mixture onto each lettuce leaf and sprinkle with some of the peanuts. Fold the sides over the filling and roll to enclose. Pass with additional soy sauce for dipping.

Sensation Salad

Serves 8

Garlic Vinaigrette

7 garlic cloves

7 tablespoons red wine vinegar

1 1/2 teaspoons salt

1 1/2 cups vegetable oil

1 1/2 cups olive oil

Salad

3 heads lettuce, trimmed and torn into bite-size pieces

1/2 cup (2 ounces) freshly grated Romano cheese

4 ounces blue cheese, crumbled

1 cup chopped fresh parsley

1 cup cherry tomato halves

1/2 cup sliced red onion

*F*or the vinaigrette, combine the garlic, vinegar and salt in a bowl and mix well. Add the vegetable oil and olive oil gradually, whisking constantly until incorporated. Pour into a 1-quart jar with a tight-fitting lid and chill for 24 hours. Shake and discard the garlic before serving.

For the salad, toss the lettuce, Romano cheese, blue cheese, parsley, tomatoes and onion in a salad bowl. Add the desired amount of vinaigrette and mix until coated. Freezing cheese for 1 hour prior to use makes the grating process easier.

*W*est Coast Turf was founded in 1990 with the aim of providing the best sod and service in the business. We offer more than twenty different varieties of fresh, top-quality sod along with such services as expert installation and worldwide shipping. Our attractive, durable grasses—St. Augustine, hybrid and improved common Bermuda, bentgrass, bluegrass, rye, zoysia, fescue, and seashore paspalum—are the sod of choice by homeowners, school districts, parks and recreation facilities, and sports turf managers across the nation and around the world.

Hot Grain Salad

Serves 8

3 cups water
1 tablespoon chicken bouillon granules
1/2 cup black or regular quinoa
1/2 cup millet
1/2 cup white rice
2 tablespoons olive oil
1/2 red bell pepper, chopped
1/2 yellow bell pepper, chopped
1/2 orange bell pepper, chopped
3 garlic cloves, minced
2 shallots, minced
1/2 cup cooked lima beans, black beans or soy beans
2 green onions, chopped
1 teaspoon hot sauce
Soy sauce to taste
Apple cider vinegar to taste
Salt and pepper to taste

*B*ring the water and bouillon granules to a boil in a 4-quart saucepan. Stir in the quinoa, millet and rice. Return to a boil and reduce the heat. Simmer for 15 to 20 minutes or until the grains are tender, stirring occasionally. Cool for 8 to 10 hours if possible.

Heat the olive oil in a wok or skillet. Sauté the bell peppers, garlic and shallots in the hot oil until tender. Stir in the cooked grains. Add the lima beans, green onions and hot sauce and mix well. Splash with soy sauce and vinegar and season with salt and pepper. Serve immediately.

Chicken, Cantaloupe and Dill Salad

Serves 4

Creamy Chutney Dressing
1 cup nonfat plain yogurt
1/4 cup mayonnaise or reduced-fat mayonnaise
1 tablespoon chutney

Salad
1 large ripe cantaloupe
1 pound poached boneless skinless chicken breasts, cut into 1/2-inch pieces
3/4 cup chopped celery
1/3 cup finely chopped red onion
1/4 cup finely chopped fresh dill weed
Salt and pepper to taste
1/3 cup slivered almonds, toasted

For the dressing, combine the yogurt, mayonnaise and chutney in a bowl and mix well.

For the salad, cut the cantaloupe into halves and remove the seeds. Remove the rind and cut the cantaloupe into 1/3-inch pieces. This should equal about 1 pound.

Combine the cantaloupe, chicken, celery, onion and dill weed in a bowl and mix well. Add the dressing and mix until coated. Season with salt and pepper and chill, covered, in the refrigerator. Sprinkle with the almonds just before serving. To save time, substitute a purchased roasted chicken for the poached chicken breasts.

Barbecue Chicken and Grape Salad

Serves 4

Orange Dressing

1/4 cup mayonnaise or reduced-fat mayonnaise
1 tablespoon red wine vinegar
1 tablespoon orange juice
1/4 teaspoon salt

Salad

1 teaspoon onion powder
1 teaspoon paprika
1 teaspoon chili powder
1/2 teaspoon salt
1 pound boneless skinless chicken breasts
1 teaspoon olive oil
3/4 cup seedless green grape halves
3/4 cup seedless red grape halves
2/3 cup chopped celery
1/2 cup thinly sliced red onion
1/4 cup walnuts, toasted and chopped

*F*or the dressing, combine the mayonnaise, vinegar, orange juice and salt in a bowl and mix well.

For the salad, preheat the oven to 350 degrees. Mix the onion powder, paprika, chili powder and salt in a small bowl and sprinkle over the chicken. Heat the olive oil in an ovenproof skillet over medium-high heat. Sauté the chicken in the hot oil for 2 minutes per side or until brown. Bake for 10 minutes or until the chicken is tender. Remove the chicken to a bowl and chill, covered, in the refrigerator. Chop into bite-size pieces.

Combine the chicken, grapes, celery and onion in a salad bowl and mix well. Add the dressing and toss to coat. Sprinkle with the walnuts.

Flank Steak with Arugula Salad

Serves 6

1 (1¹/₂-pound) flank steak
¹/₄ cup extra-virgin olive oil
¹/₄ cup balsamic vinegar
Kosher salt and freshly ground pepper to taste
3 cups arugula
2 Belgian endive, sliced
2 cups cherry tomatoes, cut into halves
2 tablespoons olive oil
1 tablespoon balsamic vinegar
8 ounces (about) Parmesan cheese

*P*repare **Roasted Peppers** by following these simple instructions. Core the peppers and cut into large strips at least 1 inch wide. Arrange the pepper strips skin side up on a baking sheet and broil on high until the skin is blistered and charred. Immediately place the peppers in a paper bag and seal. Let stand for about five minutes. This will allow the peppers to sweat off the skin. Remove from the bag and gently rub off the skin. Avoid running the peppers under water as this will lessen their flavor.

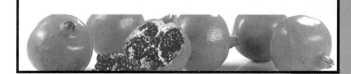

*P*lace the steak in a shallow dish. Whisk ¹/₄ cup olive oil and ¹/₄ cup vinegar in a bowl until blended and pour over the steak, turning to coat. Season with salt and pepper. Marinate in the refrigerator for 3 hours, turning occasionally.

Preheat the grill. Sear the steak over hot coals for 3 to 4 minutes on 1 side or until brown; do not turn or pierce the steak. Turn and sear for 3 to 4 minutes longer on the remaining side. Remove to a platter and let rest for 10 minutes.

To serve, toss the arugula, endive and tomatoes in a salad bowl. Drizzle with 2 tablespoons olive oil, 1 tablespoon vinegar and any collected juices from the steak and mix well. Season with salt and pepper. Slice the steak diagonally across the grain into 1¹/₂-inch-thick slices and arrange over the salad. Using a vegetable peeler, shave the cheese over the top. Serve immediately.

The image of Arizona and its cowboys are something of old Hollywood westerns to most folks. Horses, campfires, cowboy boots, gunfights—they can all still be enjoyed at themed restaurants and destinations throughout the state. Phoenicians celebrate and remember this lifestyle with the Parada del Sol ("a walk in the sun"), a month-long festival held annually in Scottsdale. Arizona was established as a state on February 14, 1912, and became known for its five c's—cattle, cotton, copper, citrus, and climate. Ranching, farming, and mining have been mainstays of the state for more than a century, and it's still evident in the laid-back attitude of Valley residents. Everything from clothing to food carries some of the casualness of the cowboys of old, reminiscing in their blue jeans next to a campfire under the stars. Go ahead, roast a marshmallow or two over the barbecue and relax.

Cowboy Casual

photo donated by 3rios fototeca
photo © Adalberto R. Lanz

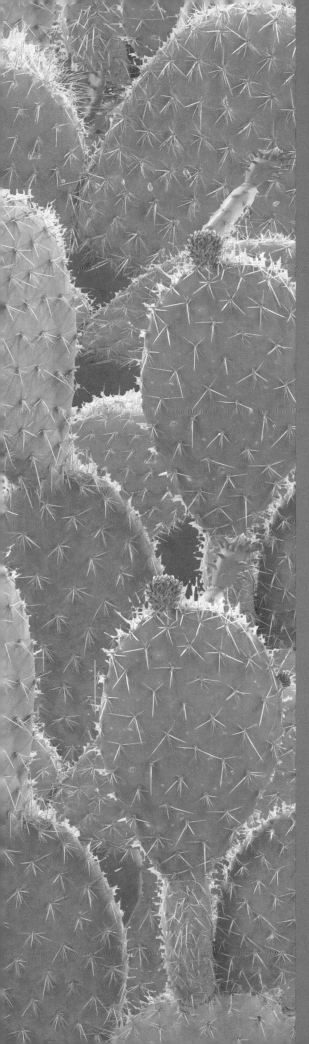

Appetizers and Soups
Arizona Dip
Chipotle Black Bean Dip
Papago Peak White Bean and Turkey Chili
Black Bean, Sausage and Hominy Stew
Wild Rice Soup
Bacon-Wrapped Shrimp with
     Smoky Barbecue Sauce

Salads
Salad Greens with Blue Cheese and
     Port Dressing
Jicama Green Leaf Salad with
     Honey Mustard Dressing
Romaine Salad with Bacon and
     Hard-Cooked Eggs

Sides
Corn Bread and Cheddar Casserole
Chipotle Macaroni and Cheese
Southwest-Style Garlic Mashed Potatoes
Grilled Vegetables

Main Courses
Gaucho-Grilled Steak with Chimichurri
Green Chile Pepper Jack Cheeseburgers
Coriander and Chili-Rubbed Lamb Chops
Roast Pork Tenderloin with
     Three-Mushroom Sauce
Ranchers' Spaghetti
Linguini with Chicken and Garlic

Desserts
Root Beer Floats
Chocolate Chip Bread Pudding
     with Whiskey Sauce
Cowboy Cookies with Vanilla Bean Ice Cream
Southwest Brownies

Cowboy Casual

ranchers' favorites

*L*ike fine food, achieving the highest standards of craftmanship starts with the combination of the right ingredients. Linthicum Custom Builders mixes experience, talent, commitment, and integrity to bring to Arizona, California, and Hawaii the craft of true custom building. Building fine architecture with the same passion with which it was designed is what sets Linthicum apart from the rest. The company is known for the strength of its people and its commitment to excellence.

Having built many of Arizona's most prized architectural statements from aggressive modernist to authentic classical styles, Linthicum builds with pride for the West's most respected architects.

Arizona Dip

Serves 12 to 15

16 ounces cream cheese, softened
1 cup sour cream
8 ounces Cheddar cheese, shredded
1 (4-ounce) can green chiles, drained and chopped
3 eggs
1 1/2 envelopes taco seasoning
1 cup sour cream
1/2 cup salsa
Guacamole

*P*reheat the oven to 350 degrees. Beat the cream cheese, 1 cup sour cream, Cheddar cheese, green chiles, eggs and taco seasoning in a mixing bowl until combined. Spoon the cream cheese mixture into a greased 8- or 9-inch springform pan and bake for 40 to 45 minutes. Cool in the pan on a wire rack for 10 minutes. Maintain the oven temperature.

Combine 1 cup sour cream and the salsa in a bowl and mix well. Spread the sour cream mixture over the top of the baked layer, starting from the outside edge of the pan. Bake for 5 minutes longer. Cool in the pan on a wire rack.

Chill, covered with waxed paper, for 8 to 10 hours. Remove the side of the pan and mound guacamole in the center. Serve with tortilla chips.

Chipotle Black Bean Dip

Chipotle chiles, canned in a spicy tomato sauce, sometimes called adobo, are available at Latin American markets, specialty markets, and some supermarkets.

Make 4 cups

2 (15-ounce) cans black beans
4 slices bacon
1 small red bell pepper, chopped
1 onion, chopped
$1/2$ teaspoon cumin
$1/2$ teaspoon oregano
1 teaspoon chopped seeded canned chipotle chile or
    jalapeño chile
Salt and pepper to taste
$1/2$ cup sour cream
2 tablespoons chopped fresh cilantro

Drain the beans, reserving the sauce. Cook the bacon in a large heavy skillet over medium heat for 6 minutes or until crisp. Drain, reserving 1 tablespoon of the pan drippings. Coarsely crumble the bacon and set aside. Sauté the bell pepper and onion in the reserved pan drippings for 6 minutes or until the onion is tender. Stir in the cumin and oregano and sauté for 1 minute. Add the beans and chipotle chile and mix well.

Simmer over medium-low heat for 5 minutes or until slightly thickened, stirring occasionally. Process 1 cup of the bean mixture in a food processor until smooth. Return the purée to the remaining bean mixture and season with salt and pepper. Adjust the consistency of the dip by adding the reserved bean sauce if desired. Spoon into a serving bowl and chill, covered, for 2 hours. You may prepare to this point up to 2 days in advance, chilling the dip and bacon separately.

Stir $1/2$ of the bacon into the chilled dip and top with the sour cream. Sprinkle with the remaining bacon and cilantro. Serve chilled or at room temperature with tortilla chips.

Papago Peak White Bean and Turkey Chili

Serves 4 to 6

1 tablespoon vegetable oil
1 onion, chopped
1 garlic clove, minced
1 poblano chile, roasted, peeled, seeded
  and chopped
2 tablespoons oregano
2 teaspoons cumin
2 teaspoons coriander
1 teaspoon cayenne pepper, or to taste
1 pound ground turkey or soy crumbles
1 (15-ounce) can Great Northern
  beans, drained

1 (14-ounce) can chicken or vegetable broth
1 (14-ounce) can diced tomatoes
1 (14-ounce) can tomato sauce
1 (11-ounce) can Shoe Peg corn, drained
Salt and black pepper to taste
Chopped green onions
Sour cream or Mexican crema
Shredded Monterey Jack cheese
Chopped fresh cilantro

*H*eat the oil in a large saucepan over medium-high heat. Sauté the onion and garlic in the hot oil for 2 minutes. Stir in the poblano chile, oregano, cumin, coriander and cayenne pepper. Sauté for 1 minute longer. Add the ground turkey and mix well.

Cook for 5 to 10 minutes or until the ground turkey is brown and crumbly, stirring frequently. Stir in the beans, broth, undrained tomatoes, tomato sauce and corn. Simmer for 30 minutes, stirring occasionally. Season with salt and black pepper and ladle into chili bowls. Garnish each serving with green onions, sour cream, cheese and cilantro.

For a thicker consistency, purée a portion of the chili in a blender and return to the saucepan. You may substitute one drained 4-ounce can diced green chiles for the poblano chile. The poblano chile will add a more spicy and smoky flavor to the chili.

Black Bean, Sausage and Hominy Stew

Serves 6

12 ounces ground turkey sausage

2 (14-ounce) cans chicken broth

1 (15-ounce) can black beans, drained and rinsed

1 (14-ounce) can golden hominy, drained and rinsed

1 (14-ounce) can Mexican-style stewed tomatoes

1 cup frozen diced hash brown potatoes

1/2 cup chopped green bell pepper

1/3 cup chopped onion

1 garlic clove, minced

1 teaspoon oregano

1/2 teaspoon chili powder

*B*rown the sausage in a large saucepan, stirring until crumbly; drain. Stir in the broth, beans, hominy, undrained tomatoes, potatoes, bell pepper, onion, garlic, oregano and chili powder. Bring to a boil; reduce the heat.

Simmer, covered, for 30 minutes, stirring occasionally. Ladle into soup bowls. You may cook in a slow cooker on Low for about 8 hours.

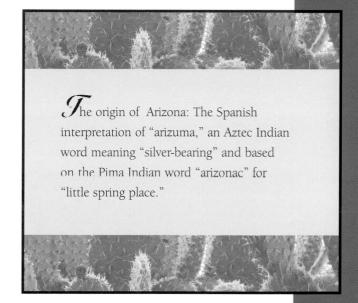

*T*he origin of Arizona: The Spanish interpretation of "arizuma," an Aztec Indian word meaning "silver-bearing" and based on the Pima Indian word "arizonac" for "little spring place."

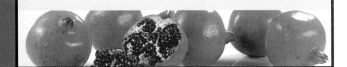

Cooking with **Prickly Pear Cactus** is easy. Just cut the spines off the pad of the cactus and cut into cubes. Steam or sauté the cactus with a little bacon and onion and season with salt and pepper to create a new side dish. We suggest that you wear padded gloves when handling cactus to prevent unintended pricks.

Wild Rice Soup

Serves 4

1¹/2 cups wild rice, rinsed
Salt to taste
9 slices bacon, chopped
1 onion, chopped
4 cups half-and-half
2 (10-ounce) cans cream of potato soup
2 cups cubed Velveeta cheese
Pepper to taste

$\mathcal{P}$reheat the oven to 500 degrees. Place the wild rice in an ovenproof glass bowl and cover with hot salted water. Cover the bowl and place on the oven rack; turn off the oven. Let stand with the door closed for 8 to 10 hours. Or, you may cook the wild rice on the stovetop using the package directions.

Sauté the bacon and onion in a large saucepan until the bacon is brown and crisp and the onion is tender; drain. Stir in the wild rice, half-and-half, soup and cheese. Simmer until the cheese melts and the soup is the desired consistency, stirring frequently. Season with salt and pepper and ladle into soup bowls.

Bacon-Wrapped Shrimp with Smoky Barbecue Sauce

Serves 8

Smoky Barbecue Sauce

1 cup soy sauce

1 cup sherry

2 tablespoons brown sugar

2 tablespoons lemon juice

1 tablespoon minced fresh gingerroot

2 teaspoons Dijon mustard

1 teaspoon liquid smoke

1 teaspoon minced garlic

1 teaspoon grated lemon zest

Shrimp

16 to 18 slices bacon, cut crosswise into halves

1 pound (32- to 36-count) shrimp, peeled
   and deveined

*F*or the sauce, bring the soy sauce, sherry, brown sugar, lemon juice, gingerroot, mustard, liquid smoke, garlic and lemon zest to a boil in a saucepan, stirring occasionally; reduce the heat. Simmer until the mixture is reduced to 1 1/2 cups and slightly thickened, stirring frequently. You may prepare up to 1 day in advance and store, covered, in the refrigerator. Reheat before use.

For the shrimp, soak 16 to 18 wooden skewers in enough water to cover in a bowl. Preheat the oven to 450 degrees. Arrange the bacon in a single layer in two 10×15-inch baking pans. Bake for 4 to 8 minutes or until the bacon begins to brown on the bottom. Drain on paper towels. Preheat the broiler.

Wrap 1 bacon half around each shrimp and secure with a soaked wooden skewer. Brush the bacon with some of the sauce and arrange on a lightly greased broiler rack in a broiler pan. Broil for 2 to 3 minutes. Turn and baste with additional sauce. Broil for 2 to 3 minutes longer or until the shrimp are opaque and the bacon is brown.

Bring the remaining barbecue sauce to a boil in a saucepan and boil for 2 minutes. Pour into a small bowl and place in the middle of a serving platter. Surround the sauce with the bacon-wrapped shrimp. You may grill the shrimp in a grill basket or on a cooking grate if desired.

Salad Greens with Blue Cheese and Port Dressing

Serves 4

Spiced Walnuts

2 egg whites
1 teaspoon salt
3/4 cup sugar
2 tablespoons paprika
2 teaspoons Worcestershire sauce
1 1/2 teaspoons cayenne pepper
4 1/2 cups walnut halves
6 tablespoons unsalted butter, melted

Port Dressing

3/4 cup dried tart cherries or cranberries
1/2 cup tawny port

5 ounces peppered bacon, chopped
2 shallots, minced
1 garlic clove, minced
1/3 cup olive oil
1/4 cup red wine vinegar
2 teaspoons sugar
1 teaspoon dry mustard
Salt and pepper to taste

Salad

5 ounces mixed salad greens
4 ounces blue cheese or Gorgonzola
   cheese, crumbled

*F*or the walnuts, preheat the oven to 325 degrees. Beat the egg whites and salt in a mixing bowl until foamy. Add the sugar, paprika, Worcestershire sauce and cayenne pepper and mix well. Fold in the walnuts and butter. Spread the walnut mixture in a single layer on a baking sheet and bake for 30 minutes, stirring occasionally. Remove to a platter to cool.

For the dressing, bring the cherries and wine to a simmer in a saucepan over medium heat, stirring occasionally. Remove from the heat and let stand for 15 minutes or until the cherries are plump. Sauté the bacon in a large heavy skillet over medium-low heat for 8 minutes or until crisp. Stir in the shallots and garlic and cook for 2 minutes, stirring frequently. Add the olive oil, vinegar, sugar and dry mustard and cook until the sugar dissolves, stirring constantly. Stir in the cherry mixture and season with salt and pepper. You may prepare up to 2 hours in advance and let stand, covered, at room temperature.

For the salad, chop enough of the walnuts to measure 1/2 cup, reserving the remaining walnuts for other uses. Toss the walnuts and salad greens in a bowl. Reheat the dressing and drizzle over the salad. Sprinkle with the blue cheese and serve immediately.

Jicama Green Leaf Salad with Honey Mustard Dressing

Serves 4

Honey Mustard Dressing

1 cup honey
1 cup Dijon mustard
1 cup white wine vinegar
1/2 cup dry white wine
1/2 cup olive oil

Salad

1 head each green and red leaf lettuce, torn into
   bite-size pieces
1 cup grated carrots
1 cup grated red radishes
1 cup julienned jicama
1 cup pine nuts, toasted
1 cup pepitas (roasted pumpkin seeds)

*F*or the dressing, combine the honey, mustard, vinegar, wine and olive oil in a food processor and process for 1 minute. Pour the dressing into a jar with a tight-fitting lid and store in the refrigerator.

For the salad, toss the green and red leaf lettuce in a bowl. Add the desired amount of dressing and mix until coated. Divide the lettuce mixture evenly among 4 salad plates. Artfully arrange the carrots, radishes, jicama, pine nuts and pepitas over the top of each salad.

*T*he Phoenix Museum of History is located in Phoenix's downtown Heritage Square. This new museum collects, preserves, interprets, and exhibits materials central to the development of Phoenix and the Salt River Valley. The museum's exhibits illustrate important milestones in the development of early Phoenix, such as when the pioneers discovered and redug the irrigation canals in the 1860s, and the historic floods and droughts. Artifacts enliven replicas of Hancock's general stores, an old ostrich farm, and a shop of Indian curios. Gain new insights into the story of how the city blossomed into a modern twentieth-century metropolis and how time and place have influenced the development of Phoenix.

Romaine Salad with Bacon and Hard-Cooked Eggs

Serves 4

2 eggs

1 large head romaine, trimmed and cut into bite-size pieces (about 1 1/4 pounds)

6 ounces bacon, cut crosswise into 1/2-inch strips (6 to 8 slices)

2 tablespoons olive oil

1/4 cup finely chopped shallots or green onions

1/4 cup red wine vinegar

1/4 teaspoon salt, or to taste

Pepper to taste

*P*lace the eggs in a small heavy saucepan and add enough water to cover by 1 inch. Partially cover the saucepan and bring to a boil. Reduce the heat to low and cook, completely covered, for 10 minutes. Immerse the eggs in a bowl of cold water to stop the cooking process. Let stand for 2 minutes or until cool enough to handle. Peel and finely chop the eggs and toss with the romaine in a bowl.

Cook the bacon in a skillet over medium heat for 8 minutes or until brown and crisp. Remove the bacon with a slotted spoon to a paper towel to drain, reserving the pan drippings. Add the olive oil and shallots to the reserved pan drippings and cook for 2 minutes or until the shallots are tender, stirring constantly. Stir in the vinegar and salt and bring to a boil. Boil for 10 seconds, swirling the skillet. Pour the hot vinaigrette over the romaine mixture and toss to coat. Mix in the bacon and season with salt and pepper.

Corn Bread and Cheddar Casserole

Serves 16

2 large onions

6 tablespoons butter

2 eggs

2 tablespoons milk

1 (16-ounce) package corn bread muffin mix

1 (14-ounce) can cream-style corn

1 cup sour cream

2 cups (8 ounces) shredded mild Cheddar cheese

*P*reheat the oven to 425 degrees. Sauté the onions in the butter in a skillet until tender. Whisk the eggs and milk in a bowl until blended and stir in the muffin mix and corn. Spread the corn bread mixture in a greased 9×13-inch baking dish. Layer with the sautéed onions and sour cream and sprinkle with the cheese. Bake for 35 minutes or until puffed and golden brown. Let stand for 10 minutes before cutting into squares.

Chipotle Macaroni and Cheese

Serves 8

1 (28-ounce) can whole tomatoes, drained
1¹/2 cups finely chopped onions
2 large garlic cloves, minced
1 to 2 tablespoons chipotle chile in adobo
¹/4 cup (¹/2 stick) unsalted butter
¹/4 cup flour
5 cups milk
Salt and pepper to taste

16 ounces elbow macaroni, cooked and drained
2 cups (8 ounces) coarsely shredded Monterey
    Jack cheese
2 cups (8 ounces) coarsely shredded
    extra-sharp Cheddar cheese
¹/4 cup fresh bread crumbs
¹/2 cup (2 ounces) freshly grated
    Parmesan cheese

*P*reheat the oven to 375 degrees. Chop the tomatoes and drain again. Sauté the onions, garlic and chipotle chile in the butter in a skillet for 5 minutes or until the onions are tender. Stir in the flour and cook for 3 minutes, stirring occasionally. Add the milk gradually, stirring constantly. Bring to a boil and stir in the tomatoes. Simmer and season with salt and pepper. Add the pasta to the tomato mixture and mix well. Stir in the Monterey Jack cheese and Cheddar cheese and spoon into a buttered 9×13-inch baking dish or 3-quart gratin dish. Toss the bread crumbs and Parmesan cheese in a bowl and sprinkle over the top. Bake on the middle oven rack for 20 to 25 minutes or until brown and bubbly.

Southwest-Style Garlic Mashed Potatoes

Serves 8

6 white potatoes, peeled and coarsely chopped
6 garlic cloves
2 sweet potatoes
4 ounces cream cheese, cubed and softened
¹/2 cup sour cream

Salt and pepper to taste
1 (10-ounce) can cream of mushroom soup
1 (14-ounce) can chicken broth
1 (4-ounce) can diced green chiles

*C*ombine the white potatoes and garlic with enough water to generously cover in a saucepan. Bring to a boil and boil until the potatoes are tender; drain. Combine the sweet potatoes with enough water to cover in a saucepan. Bring to a boil and boil until tender; drain. Peel and chop the sweet potatoes. Add the sweet potatoes to the white potatoes and mash. Add the cream cheese, sour cream, salt and pepper to the potato mixture and cook until blended and heated through, stirring frequently. Remove from the heat and cover to keep warm. Mix the soup, broth and green chiles in a saucepan and cook until heated through, stirring occasionally. Serve with the potatoes.

Grilled Vegetables

Serves 8

2 red bell peppers
2 yellow bell peppers
2 Belgian endive
1 pound button mushrooms, stems removed
1/3 cup olive oil
Kosher salt and freshly ground pepper to taste
4 small zucchini or eggplant, cut lengthwise into halves
1 pound thick asparagus spears, trimmed
8 small tomatoes
Balsamic vinegar
1 lemon, cut into wedges

*P*reheat the grill on high. Cut the bell peppers into halves, discard the seeds and membranes and cut each half into 3 long strips. Cut the endive lengthwise into quarters. Cut the mushrooms into halves and wipe with a damp cloth. Preheat a grill grate on the grill for 5 minutes.

Brush the bell peppers with some of the olive oil and sprinkle with salt and pepper. Grill on the grill grate until slightly charred on all sides. Remove the bell peppers to a platter. Brush the endive, mushrooms, zucchini, asparagus and tomatoes with some of the remaining olive oil and sprinkle with salt and pepper. Grill the vegetables on the grill grate until slightly charred, brushing with some of the remaining olive oil as needed.

Arrange the grilled vegetables in rows on a platter, varying the shapes and colors. Drizzle with the remaining olive oil and let stand until cool. Sprinkle with salt and pepper and drizzle with vinegar just before serving. Serve with the lemon wedges.

Gaucho-Grilled Steak with Chimichurri

Serves 8

Chimichurri

1/4 cup red wine vinegar
3 garlic cloves, minced
2 jalapeño chiles, minced
1 bunch fresh flat-leaf parsley, trimmed and finely chopped
1 handful fresh oregano, finely chopped
Juice of 2 limes
1 cup olive oil
1 teaspoon kosher salt
1 teaspoon crushed black peppercorns

Steak

Extra-virgin olive oil
4 pounds skirt steak, trimmed
Kosher salt and freshly ground pepper to taste

*F*or variety, substitute **Jalapeño Pesto** for the Chimichurri. Combine 3 coarsely chopped seeded large jalapeño chiles, 3 crushed large garlic cloves, 1/2 cup coarsely chopped fresh cilantro, 1/2 teaspoon cumin, 3 tablespoons lime juice and 2 to 3 tablespoons water in a food processor or blender and process until smooth. Taste and season with salt and pepper.

*F*or the chimichurri, combine the vinegar, garlic and jalapeño chiles in a bowl and mix well. Stir in the parsley, oregano and lime juice. Whisk in the olive oil until incorporated. Add the salt and peppercorns and mix well. Let stand at room temperature to allow the flavors to marry.

For the steak, preheat a charcoal grill on high. Drizzle olive oil over the steak in a shallow dish, turning to coat. Marinate at room temperature for 30 minutes, turning occasionally. Drain and generously sprinkle with salt and pepper; the seasonings should be visible.

Grill the steak over direct heat for 4 minutes per side or until charred. Remove to a cutting board and let rest for 5 minutes. Cut the steak diagonally across the grain and fan the slices on a platter. Drizzle with some of the sauce and pass the remaining sauce at the table. You may broil if desired.

Green Chile Pepper Jack Cheeseburgers

Serves 4

Poblano Sauce

4 garlic cloves

2 poblano chiles, roasted, peeled and seeded

1/4 cup water

2 tablespoons chopped fresh cilantro

Juice from 1/2 lime

1/2 teaspoon cumin

1/2 teaspoon oregano

Cheeseburgers

1 1/2 pounds ground sirloin

1 cup (4 ounces) shredded Pepper Jack cheese

Salt and pepper to taste

4 hamburger buns, split

Vegetable oil

1 poblano chile, roasted, peeled, seeded and cut into strips

*F*or the sauce, blacken the garlic in a skillet over medium-high heat. Process the garlic, poblano chiles, water, cilantro, lime juice, cumin and oregano in a blender until puréed.

For the cheeseburgers, preheat the grill on medium. Divide the ground sirloin into 4 equal portions. Place 1/4 cup of the cheese in the center of each portion and shape the ground sirloin around the cheese to form a patty. Sprinkle with salt and pepper.

Grill the patties until a meat thermometer registers 160 degrees, turning once. Brush the cut sides of the buns with oil and grill for 1 minute or until light brown. Serve the cheeseburgers on the buns topped with the poblano chile strips and the sauce. Stuff the burgers with the poblano chile strips if desired.

Coriander and Chili-Rubbed Lamb Chops

Serves 4 to 6

1/2 cup chopped fresh cilantro
6 tablespoons olive oil
3 tablespoons chili powder
2 tablespoons minced garlic
1 tablespoon cumin
1 tablespoon coriander
1 1/2 teaspoons salt
1 teaspoon freshly ground pepper
12 lamb loin chops

*C*ombine the cilantro, olive oil, chili powder, garlic, cumin, coriander, salt and pepper in a bowl and mix well. Coat the lamb chops with the cilantro mixture. Arrange the chops in a single layer on a platter and chill, covered, for 4 to 10 hours.

Oil the grill rack and position the rack 4 inches from the heat source and preheat. Arrange the lamb chops on the grill rack and grill for 5 to 7 minutes on each side for medium-rare or until the desired degree of doneness. Serve with pepper jelly. You may broil if desired.

Roast Pork Tenderloin with Three-Mushroom Sauce

Serves 6 to 8

Three-Mushroom Sauce

2 cups water
1 ounce dried porcini mushrooms
6 ounces portobello mushrooms, chopped
6 ounces shiitake mushrooms, chopped
6 tablespoons minced shallots
2 tablespoons olive oil
3 1/2 cups beef stock
3/4 cup cream sherry

Pork Tenderloin and Assembly

2 (10-ounce) pork tenderloins
Salt and pepper to taste
2 garlic cloves, minced
1 tablespoon minced fresh rosemary
1 teaspoon olive oil

*F*or the sauce, bring the water to a boil in a saucepan. Mix in the porcini mushrooms and remove from the heat. Let stand for 30 minutes to reconstitute. Drain, reserving the liquid and discarding the sediment. Chop the mushrooms. Sauté the porcini mushrooms, portobello mushrooms, shiitake mushrooms and shallots in the olive oil in a skillet until the shallots are tender. Add the reserved liquid, stock and sherry and bring to a boil. Boil for 30 minutes or until the liquids are reduced by 1/2, stirring occasionally.

For the tenderloin, preheat the oven to 425 degrees. Sprinkle the tenderloins with salt and pepper. Mix the garlic, rosemary and olive oil in a bowl and rub over the surface of the tenderloins. Arrange in a baking dish and roast for 10 minutes. Reduce the oven temperature to 375 degrees and roast for about 30 minutes longer or until a meat thermometer registers 160 degrees. Remove to a platter and tent with foil, reserving the pan drippings.

To assemble, pour the reserved pan drippings into the sauce and bring to a boil, stirring occasionally. Cut the pork into 1-inch slices and serve with the sauce.

Ranchers' Spaghetti

Serves 6 to 8

1 1/2 pounds sweet Italian sausage, casings removed and finely chopped
1 large onion, chopped
3 or 4 garlic cloves
2 (28-ounce) cans crushed tomatoes
1 (29-ounce) can tomato sauce
1 (6-ounce) can tomato paste
1 tablespoon sugar
1 1/2 teaspoons oregano
1 1/2 teaspoons basil
1 teaspoon crushed red pepper
Salt and black pepper to taste
Hot cooked pasta

Brown the sausage in a large stockpot over medium heat, stirring constantly. Remove the sausage to a platter using a slotted spoon, reserving the pan drippings. Sauté the onion in the reserved pan drippings until tender. Stir in the garlic and sauté briefly; drain. Add the undrained tomatoes, tomato sauce, tomato paste and sugar and mix well. Stir in the sausage, oregano, basil, red pepper, salt and black pepper. Bring to a boil; reduce the heat.

Simmer for 4 to 5 hours or until thickened and deep red in color, stirring occasionally. Spoon the sauce over your favorite hot cooked pasta. The flavor of the sauce is enhanced if prepared 1 day in advance and stored, covered, in the refrigerator. Reheat before serving.

This recipe may be adapted to a slow cooker. Brown the sausage, onion and garlic as stated above and spoon into a slow cooker. Add the remaining ingredients and cook on Low for 8 to 10 hours or on High for 3 to 4 hours.

Linguini with Chicken and Garlic

Serves 4

1/4 cup olive oil
1/4 cup minced garlic
12 ounces linguini
Salt to taste
1 1/2 pounds boneless skinless chicken breasts,
    cut into thin strips
2 poblano chiles, seeded and julienned

1/4 cup thinly sliced fresh basil
3 plum tomatoes, seeded and chopped
4 ounces prosciutto, chopped
2 tablespoons butter
1 cup (4 ounces) grated Parmesan cheese
Pepper to taste
1/4 cup thinly sliced fresh basil

*H*eat the olive oil in a small heavy skillet over medium heat. Cook the garlic in the hot oil for 6 minutes or until light brown. Strain, reserving the garlic and oil. Cook the pasta in boiling salted water in a saucepan until al dente. Drain and cover to keep warm.

Heat 1 tablespoon of the reserved oil in a large heavy skillet over medium-high heat. Sauté the chicken in the hot oil for 5 minutes. Add the poblano chiles and sauté for 2 minutes. Add 1/4 cup basil, the tomatoes, prosciutto and 2 tablespoons of the reserved garlic and mix well. Sauté for 1 minute or until the chicken is cooked through. Remove from the heat and stir in the butter until melted.

Toss the hot pasta, chicken mixture and 1/2 cup of the cheese in a bowl. Season with salt and pepper and sprinkle with 1/4 cup basil and the remaining 2 tablespoons reserved garlic. Serve with the remaining 1/2 cup cheese.

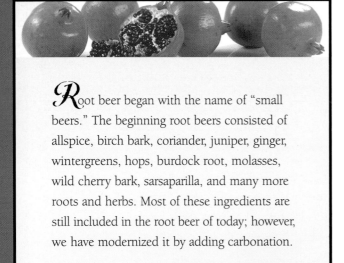

*R*oot beer began with the name of "small beers." The beginning root beers consisted of allspice, birch bark, coriander, juniper, ginger, wintergreens, hops, burdock root, molasses, wild cherry bark, sarsaparilla, and many more roots and herbs. Most of these ingredients are still included in the root beer of today; however, we have modernized it by adding carbonation.

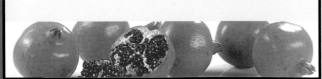

Root Beer Floats

Serves 2

1 pint vanilla ice cream
2 bottles old-fashioned root beer, chilled
Splash of bourbon (optional)
Whipped cream to taste

*S*coop the ice cream evenly into 2 tall float glasses. Pour the root beer and bourbon over the ice cream and top each with a dollop of whipped cream. Serve immediately.

Chocolate Chip Bread Pudding with Whiskey Sauce

Serves 8 to 10

Bread Pudding

8 large croissants, cut into 1-inch pieces
   (about 16 ounces)

1/2 cup (1 stick) unsalted butter, melted

1 cup (6 ounces) semisweet chocolate chips

21/2 cups half-and-half

1 cup sugar

6 eggs

4 egg yolks

2 tablespoons vanilla extract

1/8 teaspoon salt

2 tablespoons unsalted butter, melted

2 tablespoons dark brown sugar

Whiskey Sauce

11/2 cups heavy cream

2 teaspoons cornstarch

2 tablespoons cold water

1/3 cup sugar

1/3 cup whiskey

For the pudding, toss the croissants and 1/2 cup butter in a bowl until coated. Add the chocolate chips and mix well. Spread the croissant mixture over the bottom of a buttered 9×13-inch baking dish. Whisk the half-and-half, sugar, eggs, egg yolks, vanilla and salt in a bowl until blended and pour over the prepared layer. Let stand for 30 minutes, occasionally pressing the bread cubes into the custard to ensure even coverage. You may prepare to this point up to 1 day in advance and store, covered, in the refrigerator.

Preheat the oven to 350 degrees. Drizzle 2 tablespoons butter over the top of the prepared layers and sprinkle with the brown sugar. Bake for 1 hour or until puffed, brown and set in the center.

For the sauce, bring the heavy cream to a boil in a saucepan. Mix the cornstarch and water in a small bowl until smooth and whisk into the hot cream. Return to a boil; reduce the heat. Cook for 30 seconds, stirring constantly. Stir in the sugar and whiskey. Cook just until the sugar dissolves, stirring frequently. Cool to room temperature and serve with the warm bread pudding. You may substitute commercially prepared caramel sauce for the whiskey sauce.

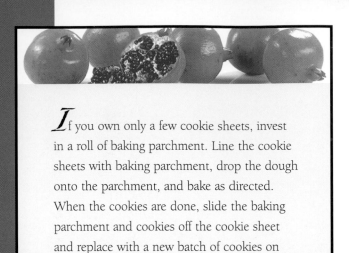

*I*f you own only a few cookie sheets, invest in a roll of baking parchment. Line the cookie sheets with baking parchment, drop the dough onto the parchment, and bake as directed. When the cookies are done, slide the baking parchment and cookies off the cookie sheet and replace with a new batch of cookies on a clean sheet of baking parchment. Makes cleanup very easy.

Cowboy Cookies with Vanilla Bean Ice Cream

Makes 3 dozen large cookies, or 6 dozen small cookies

3 cups flour
1 tablespoon baking powder
1 tablespoon baking soda
1 tablespoon cinnamon
1 teaspoon salt
1 cup butter-flavor shortening
1/2 cup (1 stick) butter, softened
1 1/2 cups packed light brown sugar
1 1/2 cups sugar
3 eggs
1 tablespoon vanilla extract
3 cups rolled oats
3 cups (18 ounces) chocolate chips, or 2 cups double
   chocolate chocolate chips
2 cups sweetened flaked coconut
2 cups chopped pecans
Vanilla bean ice cream

*P*reheat the oven to 350 degrees. Mix the flour, baking powder, baking soda, cinnamon and salt together. Beat the shortening and butter in a mixing bowl until smooth, scraping the bowl occasionally. Add the brown sugar and sugar and beat until creamy. Add the eggs and vanilla and beat until blended. Add the flour mixture and beat just until combined. Stir in the oats, chocolate chips, coconut and pecans.

Using an extra-large scoop or a 1/4-cup measure, drop the dough 3 inches apart onto an ungreased cookie sheet. Bake for 17 to 20 minutes or until the edges are light brown. Cool on the cookie sheet for 2 minutes. Remove to a wire rack to cool completely. Serve with vanilla bean ice cream. Store leftovers in an airtight container.

Southwest Brownies

For traditional brownies, omit the ancho chile powder, Saigon cinnamon, and chipotle chile powder. These spices give the rich cocoa taste a very subtle kick.

Makes 1¹/3 dozen brownies

Brownies

¹/2 cup flour
¹/2 teaspoon ancho chile powder
¹/2 teaspoon Saigon cinnamon
¹/2 teaspoon chipotle chile powder
¹/4 teaspoon salt
¹/2 cup (1 stick) plus 2 tablespoons margarine
6 tablespoons baking cocoa
1 cup sugar
1 teaspoon vanilla extract
2 eggs, lightly beaten

Chocolate Frosting

4¹/2 tablespoons baking cocoa
3 tablespoons margarine
1 cup (or more) confectioners' sugar
3 tablespoons milk
¹/2 teaspoon vanilla extract
¹/8 teaspoon salt

*F*or the brownies, preheat the oven to 350 degrees. Mix the flour, ancho chile powder, Saigon cinnamon, chipotle chile powder and salt together. Heat the margarine and baking cocoa in a saucepan over low heat until blended, stirring frequently. Remove from the heat and stir in the sugar, vanilla and eggs. Add the flour mixture and stir until smooth. Spoon the batter into a greased 8×8-inch baking pan and bake for 20 minutes. Cool in the pan on a wire rack.

For the frosting, heat the baking cocoa and margarine in a saucepan over low heat until blended, stirring frequently. Remove from the heat. Add the confectioners' sugar, milk, vanilla and salt and mix until smooth, adding additional confectioners' sugar if needed for the desired consistency. Spread the frosting over the top of the brownies. Let stand until set and cut into bars. Serve with a dollop of whipped cream or vanilla ice cream if desired.

At the end of the Mexican-American War in 1848, the United States acquired the land that is now known as Arizona. The state is home to a rich Hispanic and Native American history. The first people to inhabit what is now Arizona were Native Americans. Their culture is interwoven in everything from clothing to art, jewelry to food. Residents and visitors alike can see the ruins of the Hohokam Indians at the Pueblo Grande Museum in Phoenix. The influence of Hispanic culture is also evident in the many cultural celebrations that take place throughout the year, Cinco de Mayo being one of the most popular. And no matter where you might be in Arizona, you are never far from good Mexican food. Much of the Southwestern cuisine and culture in Arizona is a mixture of the Native American and Mexican influences. Fiestas are casual celebrations, offering family and friends time to celebrate life's big and little moments.

Fiesta Under the Sun

Cocktails
Agua de Jamaica
Cuba Libre
Mojito
Prickly Pear Margaritas

Appetizers and Soups
Bisbee Guacamole
Black Bean and Poblano Nachos
Smoked Gouda and Caramelized
      Onion Quesadillas
Clear Gazpacho
Spicy Pumpkin and Black Bean Soup

Salsas
Salsa de Bandera
Salsa de Molcajete
Tomatillo Verde Sauce with Avocado

Sides
Poblano Chile Polenta
Calabacitas Picadas con Elote
Saffron Rice

Main Courses
Pork Tenderloin with Citrus Chipotle Sauce
Chiles en Nogada with Walnut Sauce and
      Pomegranate Seeds
Pollo en Mole Verde
Ancho Chile Cheese Enchiladas
Camarones al Mojo de Ajo

Breads
Corn Tortillas
Flour Tortillas

Desserts
Flan
Crepas de Cajeta
Frozen Lime Pie

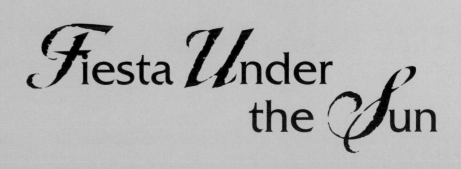

Fiesta Under the Sun

southwest traditions

Agua de Jamaica

Hibiscus flowers may be purchased by the bag in Latino markets.

Serves 6 to 8

2 cups dried Jamaica (hibiscus) flowers
10 cups water
3/4 cup sugar

*R*inse the flowers to remove any impurities. Combine the flowers and 6 cups of the water in a saucepan and bring to a boil; reduce the heat to medium. Cook for 10 minutes. Remove from the heat and let stand for 10 to 20 minutes.

Strain the flower mixture into a pitcher, discarding the flowers. Add the remaining 4 cups water and sugar and mix well. Chill, covered, until serving time. Pour over ice in glasses.

Cuba Libre

Serves 1

1 1/2 ounces light rum
Ice
Coca-Cola
Juice of 1/2 lime
1 lime slice

*M*ix the rum, ice and Coca-Cola in a highball glass. Add the lime juice and mix well. Garnish with the lime slice and serve immediately.

Mojito

Serves 1

6 sprigs of fresh mint
2 tablespoons fresh lime juice
2 teaspoons sugar
Ice cubes
1¹/₂ ounces light rum
Club soda or seltzer water, chilled
1 sprig of fresh mint
1 lemon slice

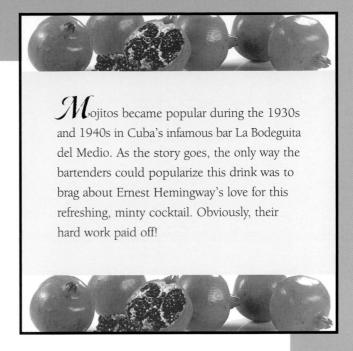

*M*ojitos became popular during the 1930s and 1940s in Cuba's infamous bar La Bodeguita del Medio. As the story goes, the only way the bartenders could popularize this drink was to brag about Ernest Hemingway's love for this refreshing, minty cocktail. Obviously, their hard work paid off!

*C*ombine 6 sprigs of mint, the lime juice and sugar in a cocktail shaker and crush with the back of a spoon until the sugar dissolves. Add ice cubes and the rum and shake until combined. Pour into a glass and top off with club soda; stir. Garnish with 1 sprig of mint and the lemon slice. You may rub the rim of the glass with a lime wedge and dip in sugar before adding the mojito.

Prickly Pear Margaritas

Prickly pear cactus syrup may be purchased at specialty supermarkets.

Serves 4

12 ounces tequila
8 ounces Triple Sec
8 ounces fresh lime juice
4 ounces prickly pear cactus syrup
2 ounces orange juice

*T*o serve on the rocks, combine the tequila, liqueur, lime juice, cactus syrup and orange juice in a cocktail shaker and shake to mix. Pour over ice in margarita glasses.

To serve blended, combine 4 cups ice, the tequila, liqueur, lime juice, cactus syrup and orange juice in a blender and process until of the desired consistency. Pour into margarita glasses. Rim the margarita glasses with sugar or salt if desired.

Bisbee Guacamole

Wow your guests by preparing the guacamole in their presence using a molcajete y tejolete, a mortar and pestle made from volcanic rock. Serve in the same dish.

Serves 8

1/3 cup chopped white onion
3 or 4 serrano chiles, finely chopped, or to taste
1 teaspoon coarse salt
2 pounds ripe avocados, coarsely chopped (about 4 cups)
2 to 3 tablespoons fresh lime juice
3/4 cup finely chopped pear or peach
3/4 cup red seedless grape halves
3/4 cup pomegranate seeds (seasonal)

*M*ash the onion, serrano chiles and salt into a coarse paste using a molcajete y tejolete, or mortar and pestle. Add the avocados and mix just until of a chunky consistency. Stir in the lime juice. Fold in the pear, grapes and 1/2 cup of the pomegranate seeds. Sprinkle with the remaining pomegranate seeds and serve with tortilla chips.

Black Bean and Poblano Nachos

Serves 8

8 ounces fried or baked tortilla chips
1 (15-ounce) can black beans, heated
2 poblano chiles, roasted, peeled, seeded and chopped
1 (4-ounce) can sliced pickled jalapeño chiles
1 cup (4 ounces) finely shredded Monterey Jack cheese
1 ripe avocado, chopped
1/4 cup sour cream
1 tablespoon coarsely chopped fresh cilantro
Juice of 1/2 lime
Salt to taste
1/4 cup coarsely chopped fresh cilantro

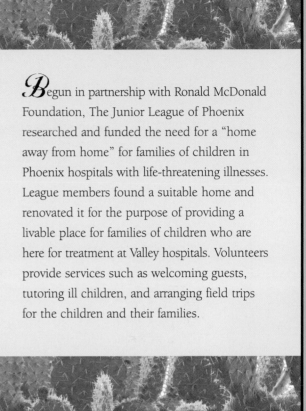

Begun in partnership with Ronald McDonald Foundation, The Junior League of Phoenix researched and funded the need for a "home away from home" for families of children in Phoenix hospitals with life-threatening illnesses. League members found a suitable home and renovated it for the purpose of providing a livable place for families of children who are here for treatment at Valley hospitals. Volunteers provide services such as welcoming guests, tutoring ill children, and arranging field trips for the children and their families.

Preheat the oven to 400 degrees. Arrange 1/2 of the tortilla chips in a large shallow baking dish or on an ovenproof platter. Top with 1/2 of the beans in small spoonfuls and sprinkle with 1/2 of the poblano chiles and 1/2 of the jalapeño chiles. Repeat the process with the remaining chips, remaining beans and remaining chiles. Sprinkle with the cheese and bake for 3 to 5 minutes or until heated through and bubbly.

Combine the avocado, sour cream, 1 tablespoon cilantro, lime juice and salt in a bowl and mix well. Top the nachos with dollops of the avocado mixture and sprinkle with 1/4 cup cilantro. Serve immediately. You may substitute one 4-ounce can diced green chiles for the poblano chiles. Add browned chorizo or browned ground beef, pork or turkey for a heartier dish, positioning the sausage or meat on top of the beans in the layering sequence.

Smoked Gouda and Caramelized Onion Quesadillas

Makes 4 quesadillas

2 tablespoons butter
1 onion, thinly sliced
1 tablespoon brown sugar
1/4 teaspoon white wine vinegar
11/2 cups (6 ounces) shredded smoked Gouda cheese
4 (10-inch) flour tortillas
2 ounces sliced prosciutto, chopped
Pepper to taste
2 tablespoons butter, melted
Chopped fresh chives
Guacamole
Sour cream

Heat 2 tablespoons butter in a heavy skillet over medium heat. Add the onion, brown sugar and vinegar to the skillet and sauté for 25 minutes or until the onion is caramelized. Remove from the heat and cool to room temperature.

Preheat the oven to 350 degrees. Sprinkle the cheese evenly over 1/2 of each tortilla. Layer the prosciutto and caramelized onion over the cheese. Sprinkle with pepper and fold to enclose the filling. Brush with some of the melted butter.

Brush a large heavy skillet with some of the melted butter and heat over medium-high heat. Cook the quesadillas in batches in the hot skillet for 2 minutes per side or until brown spots appear, brushing the skillet with some of the melted butter between batches. Arrange the quesadillas on a baking sheet and bake for 5 minutes or until the cheese melts and the tortillas are golden brown.

Cut each quesadilla into 6 wedges and sprinkle with chives. Serve hot with guacamole and sour cream. You may bake in advance and store, covered, in the refrigerator. Reheat in the oven before serving.

Clear Gazpacho

Serves 4

Tomato Water
12 large beefsteak tomatoes
10 garlic cloves, roasted
1 tablespoon salt

Gazpacho
1¹/₂ tablespoons each finely julienned jicama,
    zucchini, yellow squash, tomato and red
    bell pepper
1 tablespoon each lemon juice and olive oil
Salt and pepper to taste
1 tablespoon each chopped fennel fronds,
    fresh chervil and fresh opal basil
1¹/₂ teaspoons chopped fresh savory
1¹/₂ teaspoons chopped fresh coriander
¹/₂ teaspoon olive oil

1 avocado, scooped into Parisienne balls
24 red currant tomatoes
12 yellow currant tomatoes, cut into halves
2 tablespoons each minced peeled yellow
    plum, blanched zucchini, peeled apple
    and peeled cucumber
2 tablespoons tomato concassée
2 or 3 red jalapeño chiles, finely sliced
Snipped fresh chives to taste

*F*or the tomato water, process the tomatoes, garlic and salt in batches in a food processor until ground. Tie the ground tomato mixture in cheesecloth and place over a bowl to drain. Drain in the refrigerator for 8 to 10 hours.

For the gazpacho, toss the jicama, julienned zucchini, yellow squash, julienned tomato, bell pepper, lemon juice and 1 tablespoon olive oil in a bowl. Season lightly with salt and pepper and chill thoroughly in the refrigerator. Toss the fennel, chervil, basil, savory, coriander and ¹/₂ teaspoon olive oil in a bowl. Season lightly with a few grains of salt. Pack a 1¹/₄- to 1¹/₂-inch round cutter with the jicama mixture in the center of each of 4 soup bowls. Remove the cutter and top each round with a small mound of the fennel mixture. Divide the avocado, currant tomatoes, plum, chopped zucchini, apple, cucumber, tomato concassée and jalapeño chiles evenly among the bowls. Sprinkle with chives and add ¹/₃ cup of the Tomato Water to each bowl.

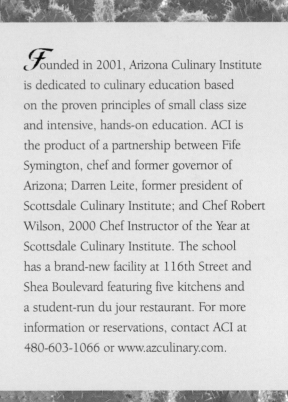

*F*ounded in 2001, Arizona Culinary Institute is dedicated to culinary education based on the proven principles of small class size and intensive, hands-on education. ACI is the product of a partnership between Fife Symington, chef and former governor of Arizona; Darren Leite, former president of Scottsdale Culinary Institute; and Chef Robert Wilson, 2000 Chef Instructor of the Year at Scottsdale Culinary Institute. The school has a brand-new facility at 116th Street and Shea Boulevard featuring five kitchens and a student-run du jour restaurant. For more information or reservations, contact ACI at 480-603-1066 or www.azculinary.com.

Spicy Pumpkin and Black Bean Soup

Serves 4 to 6

2 tablespoons New Mexico chili powder
1 teaspoon cumin seeds
1 (14-ounce) can no-salt-added diced tomatoes
1 cup coarsely chopped onion
1 (7-ounce) can fire-roasted green chiles, drained
2 garlic cloves
1 tablespoon vegetable oil
2 (15-ounce) cans black beans
1 (16-ounce) can pumpkin purée, or 2 to 3 cups chopped baked butternut squash
3 cups chicken broth
Salt to taste
Sour cream
Lime wedges
Chopped fresh cilantro

*C*ombine the chili powder and cumin seeds in a 5- or 6-quart saucepan. Cook over medium-high heat for 3 to 4 minutes or until the mixture begins to smoke, stirring frequently. Combine the chili powder mixture, undrained tomatoes, onion, green chiles, garlic and oil in a blender or food processor and process until puréed.

Return the purée to the saucepan. Simmer, partially covered, over medium-high heat for 5 to 7 minutes or until slightly thickened, stirring occasionally. Stir in the undrained beans, pumpkin purée and broth. Bring to a simmer over high heat; reduce the heat. Simmer, covered, for 10 minutes to allow the flavors to marry, stirring occasionally. Season with salt. Remove from the heat and let stand until cool.

Process the soup with a cordless blender until smooth. Reheat just until hot, stirring frequently. Ladle into soup bowls and serve with sour cream, lime wedges and cilantro. For variety, spoon the pumpkin mixture over rice.

Salsa de Bandera

Even though commonly known as Pico de Gallo, in the state of Sonora, Arizona's border state, it is known as Salsa de Bandera or Flag Salsa. The colors represent the three colors of the Mexican flag.

Makes 1 1/2 cups

3 vine-ripened tomatoes, finely chopped
1/2 cup finely chopped onion
2 to 5 serrano chiles, finely chopped

1/2 cup fresh cilantro, finely chopped
2 teaspoons salt
2 teaspoons lime juice

Drain the tomatoes in a colander. Combine the tomatoes, onion, serrano chiles, cilantro, salt and lime juice in a bowl and mix gently. Taste and adjust the seasonings and serve with tortilla chips. The flavor is enhanced if prepared at least 1 hour in advance.

Salsa de Molcajete

The name of this salsa is derived from the fact that it is traditionally made by grinding the ingredients in a molcajete, or mortar, for a chunky consistency. For entertaining, serving the salsa in a molcajete makes a nice and festive presentation.

Makes 1 1/2 cups

2 vine-ripened tomatoes
1/2 large onion, coarsely chopped
2 garlic cloves
2 poblano chiles, roasted, peeled and seeded

1 teaspoon cumin
1 teaspoon salt, or to taste
Juice of 1 Mexican lime or Key lime

Preheat the broiler. Cut the tomatoes into quarters and arrange on a baking sheet. Broil on the top oven rack for 10 to 15 minutes or until blackened, turning occasionally. Drain in a colander.

Cook the onion and garlic in a skillet over medium-high heat for 15 minutes or until blackened, stirring frequently. Combine the tomatoes, onion mixture, poblano chiles, cumin, salt and lime juice in a blender and process to the desired consistency. Taste and adjust the seasonings. Serve warm or chilled with tortilla chips.

Tomatillo Verde Sauce with Avocado

Makes 2 cups

2 to 4 serrano chiles
10 ounces tomatillos, husks removed
1 garlic clove
1 tablespoon coarsely chopped pickled jalapeño chile
1 tablespoon pickled jalapeño chile vinegar
1/2 cup fresh cilantro, coarsely chopped
1 teaspoon salt
1 avocado, chopped
1/3 cup finely chopped onion

*B*ring a saucepan of water to a boil and add the serrano chiles. Boil for 5 minutes and add the tomatillos. Boil for 5 minutes longer and remove from the heat; drain.

Combine the serrano chiles, tomatillos, garlic, jalapeño chile and vinegar in a blender and process until puréed. Add the cilantro and salt and process until blended. Combine the purée, avocado and onion in a bowl and mix well. Taste and adjust the seasonings and serve with tortilla chips.

Poblano Chile Polenta

Serves 6

2 poblano chiles, roasted, peeled and seeded
2 cups (about) water
1/2 cup heavy cream
1 teaspoon cumin
3 tablespoons unsalted butter
2 teaspoons salt
1 1/2 cups instant polenta
1/2 cup Mexican crema or sour cream
1/2 cup chopped fresh cilantro

*C*ut the poblano chiles into thick slices. Combine the poblano chile slices, water, heavy cream and cumin in a blender and process until smooth. Pour the chile mixture into a saucepan and bring to a boil. Stir in the butter and salt. Add the polenta gradually, stirring constantly. Cook for 3 minutes or until the polenta grains have softened, stirring frequently. Spoon the polenta mixture into a greased loaf pan. Chill, covered, until firm.

Preheat a grill. Invert the polenta onto a hard surface and cut into 1-inch slices. Grill the slices over hot coals for 2 minutes per side or until grill marks appear, turning once. Serve with the Mexican crema and cilantro.

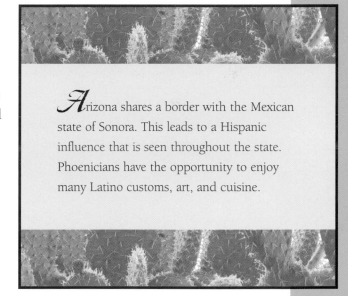

*A*rizona shares a border with the Mexican state of Sonora. This leads to a Hispanic influence that is seen throughout the state. Phoenicians have the opportunity to enjoy many Latino customs, art, and cuisine.

Calabacitas Picadas con Elote

Serves 6

2 tablespoons vegetable oil
1/4 onion, chopped
1 garlic clove, minced
1 1/2 pounds zucchini, chopped (about 6 cups)
1 cup fresh or drained canned corn

2 tomatoes, chopped
Salt and pepper to taste
1/2 cup (2 ounces) shredded cheese, such as
   Monterey Jack cheese or manchego cheese
1/4 cup chopped fresh cilantro

*H*eat the oil in a skillet over medium-high heat. Sauté the onion and garlic in the hot oil for 2 minutes. Add the zucchini and corn and sauté for 2 minutes longer. Stir in the tomatoes. Cook over high heat until the mixture begins to bubble, stirring frequently. Season with salt and pepper. Stir in the cheese and cover. Cook for 5 minutes or until the zucchini is tender, stirring occasionally. Sprinkle with the cilantro. You may substitute a mixture of yellow squash and zucchini for the zucchini.

Saffron Rice

Serves 8

3/4 cup dry white wine
1 teaspoon whole saffron threads, crumbled
3 tablespoons butter
1 1/2 cups chopped onions
2 1/4 cups long grain rice
3 3/4 cups chicken or vegetable broth
Salt and pepper to taste

3 cups thinly sliced onions
Butter to taste
1/2 cup (2 ounces) shredded Monterey Jack
   cheese or Cheddar cheese
1/2 cup Mexican crema or thick cream
1/4 cup chopped fresh parsley or cilantro

*M*ix the wine and saffron in a bowl and let stand for 5 minutes. Heat 3 tablespoons butter in a large saucepan over medium heat. Sauté the chopped onions in the butter for 5 minutes or until tender. Stir in the rice and cook for 10 to 15 minutes or until the rice begins to brown. Stir in the wine mixture and simmer until most of the liquid evaporates, stirring frequently. Add the broth and bring to a boil. Reduce the heat to low and cook, covered, for 20 minutes or until the liquid is absorbed. Season with salt and pepper. Preheat the oven to 350 degrees. Sauté the sliced onions in butter to taste in a skillet for 5 minutes. Arrange 1/2 of the rice mixture in a greased ring mold. Sprinkle with the cheese and 1/2 of the sliced onions and spread with the remaining rice mixture. Baked, covered with foil, for 10 minutes. Invert onto a platter. Spoon the Mexican crema into the center and top with the remaining sliced onions. Sprinkle with the parsley.

Pork Tenderloin with Citrus Chipotle Sauce

Serves 10

Pork Tenderloin

3¹/₂ pounds pork tenderloin
2 cups orange juice
1 cup lime juice
2 teaspoons salt
2 tablespoons unsalted butter

Citrus Chipotle Sauce

2 tablespoons unsalted butter
3 large shallots, minced
2 cups dry white wine
3 cups orange juice
2³/₄ cups chicken broth
1 cup lime juice
2 tablespoons chopped fresh cilantro
1 tablespoon chopped fresh chives
1 tablespoon chopped fresh Italian parsley
¹/₂ to 1 tablespoon minced canned
    chipotle chiles
2 tablespoons Mexican crema or heavy
    cream (optional)
Salt and pepper to taste

*F*or the pork, divide the pork evenly between 2 resealable plastic bags. Add 1 cup of the orange juice, ¹/₂ cup of the lime juice and 1 teaspoon of the salt to each bag and seal tightly. Turn to coat. Marinate in the refrigerator for 3 to 10 hours, turning occasionally; drain.

Preheat the oven to 350 degrees. Heat the butter in a large ovenproof skillet or Dutch oven. Brown the pork in the butter for 10 minutes or until brown on all sides, turning occasionally. Bake for 10 minutes or until a meat thermometer inserted in the thickest portion of the pork registers 160 degrees for medium. Remove from the oven and let stand for 10 minutes. Slice as desired.

For the sauce, heat the butter in a large saucepan over medium heat. Sauté the shallots in the butter for 2 minutes. Add the wine and cook for 10 minutes or until reduced to a glaze consistency, stirring frequently. Stir in the orange juice, broth and lime juice. Bring to a boil and boil for 45 minutes or until thickened, stirring frequently. You may prepare to this point up to 1 day in advance and store, covered, in the refrigerator. Bring to a simmer and stir in the cilantro, chives, parsley, chipotle chiles and Mexican crema. Season with salt and pepper. Serve warm with the sliced pork.

Chiles en Nogada with Walnut Sauce and Pomegranate Seeds

Makes 1 dozen chiles

Chiles en Nogada

12 poblano chiles, roasted and peeled

3 tablespoons vegetable oil

1/2 onion, finely chopped

1 garlic clove, minced

1 pear, peeled and finely chopped

1 Granny Smith apple or other variety, peeled
   and finely chopped

2 peaches, peeled and finely chopped

8 ounces each ground veal and ground pork

1 (14-ounce) can diced tomatoes

1 cup chicken stock

1/3 cup almonds, blanched and chopped

1/4 cup each raisins and brandy (optional)

1/4 teaspoon each ground cloves
   and cumin

1/4 teaspoon each cinnamon and sugar

1/16 teaspoon saffron (optional)

Salt and pepper to taste

Apple cider vinegar to taste

Walnut Sauce and Assembly

1 cup walnut halves

11/2 cups milk

1 cup cream or Mexican crema

6 ounces queso fresco or feta cheese

2 to 3 tablespoons sugar

1/4 teaspoon cinnamon

1/4 cup brandy

Salt to taste

Seeds from 2 ripe pomegranates

2 tablespoons finely chopped fresh parsley

*F*or the chiles, make a vertical slit down the side of each chile and remove the seeds carefully, leaving the stem intact. Heat the oil in a large heavy skillet over medium heat. Sauté the onion and garlic in the hot oil for 2 to 3 minutes or until the onion is tender. Stir in the pear, apple and peaches and sauté for 2 to 3 minutes. Add the ground veal and ground pork and cook for 5 to 7 minutes or until crumbly, stirring frequently. Add the undrained tomatoes, stock, almonds, raisins and brandy and mix well. Stir in the cloves, cumin, cinnamon, sugar and saffron.

Cook until the liquid evaporates and the pork and veal are cooked through, stirring constantly. Season with salt and pepper and add vinegar; cool. You may substitute 1 pound pork for the 8 ounces veal and 8 ounces pork. Preheat the oven to 200 degrees. Stuff the poblano chiles with the ground veal mixture and arrange on an ovenproof platter; tent loosely with foil. Keep warm in the oven.

For the sauce, place the walnuts in a heatproof bowl and cover with boiling water. Let stand for 5 minutes. Drain and peel the thin skin from the walnuts; this step is optional. Cover the walnuts with 1 cup of the milk and let stand for 30 to 60 minutes. Drain, discarding the milk. Process the walnuts, remaining 1/2 cup milk, cream, cheese, sugar, cinnamon and brandy in a blender until mixed. Season with salt and additional sugar and cinnamon if needed. Drizzle the sauce over the stuffed chiles and sprinkle with the pomegrante seeds and parsley.

Pollo en Mole Verde

Epazote is a fresh herb that can be found in Latino markets. Its flavor is strong, acidic, and lemony. The most common use of epazote is to flavor beans and sauces.

Serves 6

3 whole chicken breasts, split
1 carrot, sliced
1 yellow onion, sliced
1 garlic clove
1 teaspoon salt
4 peppercorns
3/4 cup pumpkin seeds, ground
8 tomatillos, cut into quarters
2 serrano chiles, chopped
1 yellow onion, cut into quarters
1 garlic clove
3 sprigs of cilantro
3 sprigs of epazote
1 tablespoon vegetable oil
Salt and pepper to taste

*C*ombine the chicken, carrot, 1 onion, 1 garlic clove, 1 teaspoon salt and peppercorns with enough water to cover in a large saucepan. Cover and bring to a boil; reduce the heat. Simmer for 15 to 20 minutes or until the chicken is tender. Remove from the heat and let stand until cool, reserving the solids and broth.

Combine 1 cup of the reserved broth, the pumpkin seeds, tomatillos, serrano chiles, 1 onion, 1 garlic clove, cilantro and epazote in a blender and process until puréed. Simmer the purée in the oil in a saucepan for 10 minutes, stirring frequently. Stir in 2 more cups of the reserved broth and simmer for 30 minutes longer, stirring occasionally. Season with salt and pepper to taste.

Chop the chicken into bite-size pieces, discarding the skin and bones. Add the chicken and remaining reserved solids to the sauce mixture and simmer until heated through, stirring frequently. Serve over hot cooked rice with tortillas. Leftovers may be served as burritos.

Ancho Chile Cheese Enchiladas

Serves 4 to 6

Ancho Chile Sauce
4 cups chicken stock
4 large ancho chiles, stemmed and seeded
2 tablespoons corn oil
1 large yellow onion, chopped
3 garlic cloves, chopped
2 tablespoons corn oil
2 tablespoons flour
4 teaspoons cumin

1 tablespoon sugar
1 1/2 teaspoons oregano
Salt and pepper to taste

Enchiladas
1 1/2 cups corn oil
12 corn tortillas
5 cups (20 ounces) shredded Monterey
    Jack cheese

*F*or the sauce, bring the stock and ancho chiles to a boil in a medium saucepan over medium-high heat; reduce the heat to medium-low. Simmer for 10 minutes or until the chiles are tender. Remove from the heat, reserving the chiles and cooking liquid.

Heat 2 tablespoons corn oil in a medium skillet over medium-high heat. Add 2/3 of the onion and cook for 3 to 5 minutes or just until it begins to soften, stirring constantly. Combine the sautéed onion, reserved chiles, 1 cup of the reserved cooking liquid and garlic in a blender and process until the consistency of a smooth paste.

Heat 2 tablespoons corn oil in a large skillet over medium heat. Whisk in the flour until blended. Cook for 2 minutes, stirring constantly with a wooden spoon. Add the reserved chile paste, cumin, sugar, oregano, remaining reserved cooking liquid, salt and pepper and mix well. Reduce the heat to medium-low and simmer for 30 minutes or until thickened, stirring frequently. Cover the sauce and keep warm over low heat.

For the enchiladas, preheat the oven to 400 degrees. Heat 1 1/2 cups corn oil in a deep skillet over medium heat until hot but not smoking. Fry the tortillas 1 at a time in the hot oil for 2 seconds per side, turning once. Immediately dip the tortillas into the chile sauce to coat. Place the tortillas on a large plate and sprinkle 1/4 cup of the cheese over the bottom third of each tortilla. Roll to enclose the cheese and arrange seam side down in a single layer in a baking dish. Spoon the remaining chile sauce over the enchiladas and sprinkle with the remaining 2 cups cheese and remaining onions. Bake for 10 minutes or until the cheese melts.

Camarones al Mojo de Ajo

Serves 6

3 garlic cloves	5 tablespoons butter
3/4 teaspoon salt	3 tablespoons olive oil
3/4 teaspoon pepper	12 garlic cloves, minced
3/4 teaspoon white vinegar	3 tablespoons lime juice
36 deveined peeled shrimp	Salt and pepper to taste

*C*ombine 3 garlic cloves, 3/4 teaspoon salt, 3/4 teaspoon pepper and the vinegar in a blender and process until puréed. Toss the shrimp with the purée in a shallow dish. Marinate, covered, in the refrigerator for 30 minutes or longer.

Heat the butter and olive oil in a skillet. Add the minced garlic to the butter mixture and sauté until golden brown. Stir in the shrimp mixture and reduce the heat. Cook, covered, until the shrimp turn pink, stirring occasionally. Drizzle with the lime juice and season with salt and pepper to taste. Spoon over hot cooked rice and garnish with chopped fresh parsley and chopped tomatoes.

Corn Tortillas

Makes 16 (5- to 6-inch) tortillas

2 cups loosely packed Maseca instant corn masa mix
1 1/8 cups water

*M*ix the masa mix and water in a bowl for 2 to 3 minutes or until the mixture forms a ball. Add an additional 1 to 2 tablespoons (or more) water if the dough feels too dry. Knead for 2 to 3 minutes or until smooth and slightly sticky. Divide the dough into 16 equal portions using a bench knife or similar utensil and shape each portion into a ball. Cover with a damp cloth to keep the dough moist.

Preheat a griddle. Flatten the balls between hands and place individually between 2 sheets of waxed paper or heavy-duty plastic wrap. Roll the dough on a hard surface or press in a tortilla press until 5 to 6 inches in diameter. Carefully remove the waxed paper or heavy-duty plastic wrap. Cook on the hot griddle for 30 to 60 seconds per side, turning once. You may store in a resealable plastic bag or wrapped in foil in the refrigerator for up to 1 week. Let the tortillas cool before frying in oil to form tostada shells.

Flour Tortillas

Makes 1 dozen (7-inch) tortillas

2 cups flour
$^1/_4$ cup shortening, butter or lard, chilled and cut into chunks
$^2/_3$ cup (or more) warm water
2 teaspoons salt

*P*rocess the flour and shortening in a food processor until crumbly. Mix the warm water and salt in a bowl and stir until the salt dissolves. Add the salt water mixture to the flour mixture and process until incorporated, adding additional warm water if needed until the mixture forms a ball.

Knead the dough on a lightly floured surface for 3 to 5 minutes or until smooth and elastic and slightly sticky. Divide the dough into 12 equal portions for 7-inch tortillas or 4 equal portions for 10-inch tortillas using a bench knife or similar utensil. Shape each portion into a ball. Let stand, covered with plastic wrap, for 30 to 60 minutes. Flatten the balls between hands and place individually between 2 sheets of waxed paper or heavy-duty plastic wrap.

Preheat a griddle over moderate heat. Using a tortilla press, press each dough portion into a 6- to 7-inch round or roll to the desired size on a hard surface. Carefully remove the waxed paper or heavy-duty plastic wrap. Cook the rounds on the hot griddle for 1 to 2 minutes per side or until puffy and golden brown, turning once. Wrap each tortilla in a damp tea towel, stacking and enclosing them in the towel as they are done. The tortillas may be wrapped in foil and stored in the refrigerator for up to 1 week.

Flan

Serves 6 to 8

1 cup sugar
1 (14-ounce) can sweetened condensed milk
1 sweetened condensed milk can milk
3 eggs
2 teaspoons vanilla extract

Spread the sugar in a heavy skillet and cook over medium-high heat until the sugar begins to melt. Swirl the skillet over the heat for 10 minutes or until the syrup darkens to a medium amber color; do not stir. Watch carefully, as caramelizing sugar darkens fast and can quickly burn. Remove from the heat and immediately pour into an 8 inch ring mold, tilting the mold so that the caramel evenly coats the bottom and slightly up the side. Place the mold in a roasting pan.

Preheat the oven to 325 degrees. Bring a saucepan of water to a boil. Remove from the heat and cover to keep hot. Combine the condensed milk, milk, eggs and vanilla in a blender and process until blended. Pour the milk mixture into the prepared mold.

Place the roasting pan on the center oven rack. Add enough hot water to the roasting pan to come halfway up the side of the mold. Be careful not to get water into the custard. Bake for 1 to 1½ hours or until the custard is barely set and just jiggles slightly. Let cool in the water bath. Chill for 4 to 10 hours, preferably overnight.

To serve, run a sharp knife around the perimeter of the mold to loosen the flan. Place a dessert plate on top of the flan and invert, allowing the caramel to run down the side. You may bake in 6 to 8 ramekins for 30 to 45 minutes if desired.

Crepas de Cajeta

Cajeta is also known as dulce de leche and can be purchased in most grocery stores. If cajeta is not available, caramel or burnt caramel is a good substitute.

Serves 6

Crepes
1¹/₂ cups milk
¹/₂ cup flour
1 egg
1 tablespoon vegetable oil
¹/₈ teaspoon salt
Butter

Orange Sauce and Assembly
2 tablespoons butter
1 cup cajeta
¹/₂ cup orange juice
1 tablespoon white tequila
³/₄ cup chopped walnuts

*F*or the crepes, beat the milk, flour, egg, oil and salt in a mixing bowl until blended. Let rest for 5 minutes. Lightly butter a nonstick crepe pan or medium skillet and heat over medium heat. Using a 1-ounce ladle, pour 2 ounces of the batter into the heated crepe pan and tilt the pan to ensure even coverage. Cook until the edge of the crepe begins to dry out and turn. Cook until the remaining side is light brown and invert onto a plate. Repeat the process approximately 11 more times with the remaining batter, buttering the crepe pan before preparing each crepe.

For the sauce, heat the butter in a small saucepan and stir in the cajeta and orange juice. Cook over medium heat for 3 to 5 minutes or until heated through, stirring constantly. Add the tequila and heat briefly. Remove from the heat, ignite with a long match and allow the flames to subside.

To assemble, fold each crepe into halves and fold again to form a triangle. Dip each of the crepes into the sauce. Arrange 2 crepes on each dessert plate and drizzle evenly with the remaining sauce. Sprinkle with the walnuts and serve immediately.

Frozen Lime Pie

Very refreshing dessert and pairs well as an ending to a Mexican or Southwestern dinner.

Serves 8 to 12

Graham Cracker Crust
1¹/2 cups graham cracker crumbs
  (about 10 crackers)
¹/4 cup sugar
6 tablespoons unsalted butter, melted

Lime Filling
6 extra-large egg yolks, at room temperature
³/4 cup fresh lime juice (6 to 8 limes)

1 (14-ounce) can sweetened condensed milk
¹/4 cup sugar
2 tablespoons grated lime zest

Topping
1 cup whipping cream, chilled
¹/4 cup sugar
¹/4 teaspoon vanilla extract
Thin lime wedges

*F*or the crust, preheat the oven to 350 degrees. Combine the graham cracker crumbs, sugar and butter in a bowl and mix well. Press the crumb mixture over the bottom and up the side of a 9-inch pie plate. Bake for 10 minutes. Cool on a wire rack.

For the filling, whisk the egg yolks and ¹/2 cup of the lime juice in a bowl and pour into a double boiler over boiling water. Cook until the mixture registers 140 degrees on a thermometer, whisking constantly; the mixture will be thick and creamy. Combine the lime mixture with the remaining ¹/4 cup lime juice, condensed milk, sugar and lime zest in a mixing bowl. Beat at medium speed for 3 minutes or until combined. Pour into the pie shell and freeze for 1¹/2 to 2 hours.

For the topping, beat the whipping cream in a mixing bowl until soft peaks form. Add the sugar and vanilla and mix well. Spoon or pipe the whipped cream over the top of the frozen layer, sealing to the edge. Freeze for 2 hours or longer before serving. Garnish each serving with lime wedges. You may freeze, wrapped in plastic wrap, for up to 3 months.

The Junior League of Phoenix believes that strong families are the foundation of a viable community. The Valley of the Sun nurtures our children's unique creative needs through its various art, science, and history programs, many of which the League contributes to both through volunteerism and financial means. Our volunteers have helped develop and staff child-friendly museums such as the Phoenix Family Museum, the Arizona Science Center, and the Phoenix Museum of History, where children are encouraged to participate in the many hands-on exhibits. Take your imagination home with you as you share the joy of cooking with your children.

Eat with Your Hands

photo donated by 3rios fototeca
photo © Adalberto R. Lanz

Appetizers
Black Bean Dip
Granny Smith Apple Spread
Avocado Sandwiches

Brunch
Early Morning French Toast
Awesome Coffee Cake
Blueberry Buttermilk Pancakes
Raspberry Waffles

Sides
Vegetable Medley
Corn Pudding
Broiled Baby Zucchini Boats with Parmesan Crust
Plentiful Potatoes

Main Courses
Messy Georges
Barbecue Cups
All-in-One Dinosaur Dinner
Stromboli with Honey Mustard Dipping Sauce

Desserts
Apple Dumplings
Popcorn Cake
Chocolate Sheet Cake
Toffee Crunch Candy
Everything Cookies
Peanut Butter Marshmallow Treats

Seasonal Desserts
Patriotic Popsicles
Cinnamon Pull
Pumpkin Roll
Cream Cheese Cookies with Royal Icing

Eat with Your Hands

fun for kids of all ages

Black Bean Dip

Serves 8 to 10

2 (16-ounce) cans black beans, drained and rinsed
2 (16-ounce) cans whole kernel corn, drained and rinsed
2 (10-ounce) cans diced tomatoes with green chiles, drained
1 red or sweet onion, chopped
Chopped green onions (optional)
2/3 cup vegetable oil or olive oil
1/2 cup apple cider vinegar
2 envelopes Italian dressing mix
Tabasco sauce to taste

*C*ombine the beans, corn, tomatoes with green chiles, red onion and green onions in a bowl and mix well. Add the oil, vinegar, dressing mix and Tabasco sauce and toss to coat. Serve with scoop corn chips. You may add commercially prepared salsa to the dip if desired.

Granny Smith Apple Spread

Serves 16

16 ounces cream cheese, softened
1 cup chopped peeled Granny Smith apple
1/2 teaspoon cinnamon
1/2 cup chopped pecans, toasted

*C*ombine the cream cheese, apple and cinnamon in a food processor and process until combined. Shape the cream cheese mixture into a ball and coat with the pecans. Chill, wrapped in plastic wrap, for 8 to 10 hours. Serve with vanilla wafers.

Avocado Sandwiches

Serves 2

1 ripe avocado
1 teaspoon finely chopped
   green onion tops
1 teaspoon parsley
1/4 teaspoon lemon juice
1/8 teaspoon dill weed

1/8 teaspoon salt, or to taste
4 slices whole wheat bread
Cream cheese, softened
   (optional)
Alfalfa sprouts

*P*eel and mash the avocado in a bowl. Stir in the green onion tops, parsley, lemon juice, dill weed and salt. Spread 1 side of each bread slice with cream cheese. Spread the avocado mixture over the cream cheese on 2 slices of the bread, sprinkle with alfalfa sprouts and top with the remaining bread slices cream cheese side down. For variety, cut the sandwiches into fun shapes with cookie cutters.

*W*e demonstrate our commitment by our beliefs:

- Funding activities and projects to make a significant impact in our community!
- Actively contributing to our community through the power of trained volunteers and a focused vision!
- Matching women of all backgrounds to work toward a common goal!
- Inspiring people to be their best!
- Lifting the spirits of those we assist!
- Yearning to leave our community stronger due to our efforts!

Early Morning French Toast

Serves 8 to 12

1/2 cup (1 stick) butter or margarine
11/2 cups packed brown sugar
1 teaspoon cinnamon
8 to 10 slices whole wheat bread

8 or 9 eggs
13/4 to 2 cups milk
1/8 teaspoon salt

*H*eat the butter in a saucepan until melted. Remove from the heat and stir in the brown sugar and cinnamon. Pour the brown sugar mixture into a 9×13-inch baking pan, tilting the pan to ensure even coverage. Arrange the bread slices over the prepared layer.

Whisk the eggs, milk and salt in a bowl until blended and pour over the bread. Chill, covered, for 8 to 10 hours. Preheat the oven to 350 degrees. Bake for 45 minutes or until light brown. Cut into squares and invert onto serving plates.

Awesome Coffee Cake

Serves 12 to 16

Walnut Filling
1 cup finely chopped walnuts or pecans
1/2 cup sugar
2 teaspoons cinnamon

Coffee Cake
1 (2-layer) package yellow cake mix with pudding
1 (4-ounce) package French vanilla or vanilla instant pudding mix
3/4 cup cold water
3/4 cup canola or vegetable oil
4 eggs
1 1/2 teaspoons butter extract
1 teaspoon vanilla extract

Confectioners' Sugar Glaze
1 cup confectioners' sugar
1 tablespoon milk
1 1/2 teaspoons vanilla extract
1 teaspoon butter extract

*F*or the filling, combine the walnuts, sugar and cinnamon in a bowl and mix well.

For the coffee cake, preheat the oven to 350 degrees. Combine the cake mix, pudding mix, cold water and canola oil in a mixing bowl and beat a medium speed until blended. Add the eggs 1 at a time, beating well after each addition. Beat at high speed for 5 minutes. Add the flavorings and beat for 1 minute longer.

Spoon 1/2 of the batter into a bundt pan sprayed with nonstick cooking spray. Sprinkle the filling over the prepared layer and spread with the remaining batter. Bake for 45 to 55 minutes or until golden brown. Cool on a wire rack for 20 minutes and invert onto a cake plate.

For the glaze, sift the confectioners' sugar into a bowl. Add the milk and flavorings and whisk until smooth. Brush the glaze over the warm cake using a pastry brush. Let stand until cool.

Blueberry Buttermilk Pancakes

Makes 20 pancakes

2 cups flour
1¹/₂ teaspoons baking soda
1¹/₂ teaspoons baking powder
¹/₂ teaspoon salt
2¹/₂ cups buttermilk

2 eggs
¹/₄ cup (¹/₂ stick) butter or margarine, melted
1 cup fresh blueberries
Vegetable oil

*M*ix the flour, baking soda, baking powder and salt in a bowl. Whisk the buttermilk, eggs and butter in a bowl until blended. Add the egg mixture to the flour mixture and mix until smooth. Fold in the blueberries. Heat a nonstick griddle or a 12-inch nonstick skillet over medium heat. Coat the hot griddle lightly with oil and adjust the heat to 350 degrees. Pour the batter by ¹/₃ cupfuls onto the hot griddle and cook for 2 minutes or until the pancakes are brown on the bottom and the edges appear dry; turn. Cook until brown on the remaining side. Repeat the process with the remaining batter, coating the griddle as needed with additional oil. Serve with butter, confectioners' sugar and/or blueberry syrup.

Raspberry Waffles

Makes 7 waffles

Raspberry Sauce
2 cups frozen raspberries
¹/₂ cup sugar

Waffles
¹/₂ to 1 cup frozen raspberries
2 cups baking mix

¹/₄ cup wheat germ
1 cup milk
2 eggs, beaten
2 tablespoons butter, melted
1 teaspoon vanilla extract
¹/₂ cup chopped walnuts

*F*or the sauce, stew the raspberries and sugar in a saucepan over low heat, stirring occasionally; slightly crush the raspberries. Remove from the heat and cover to keep warm.

For the waffles, preheat a waffle iron. Place the raspberries in a colander and rinse with warm water to thaw; drain. Combine the baking mix and wheat germ in a bowl and mix well. Whisk in the milk, eggs, butter and vanilla until smooth. Fold in the walnuts and raspberries. Spray the preheated waffle iron with nonstick cooking spray and add ¹/₂ cup of the batter. Cook using the manufacturer's directions. Repeat the process with the remaining batter. Serve with the warm sauce.

Vegetable Medley

Serves 6 to 8

2¹/2 cups fresh broccoli florets
2¹/2 cups fresh cauliflower florets
2¹/2 cups sliced carrots
1 (10-ounce) can cream of mushroom soup
1 (10-ounce) can cream of celery soup
1 cup (4 ounces) shredded Cheddar cheese

¹/2 cup mayonnaise
2 eggs, beaten
1 tablespoon minced onion
32 butter crackers, crushed
¹/2 cup (1 stick) butter, melted

*P*reheat the oven to 350 degrees. Steam the broccoli, cauliflower and carrots in a steamer for 5 minutes or until tender-crisp; drain. Spoon the broccoli mixture into a greased 9×13-inch baking dish.

Combine the soups, cheese, mayonnaise, eggs and onion in a bowl and mix well. Spread the soup mixture over the prepared layer. Toss the crackers and butter in a bowl and sprinkle over the top. Bake for 35 to 40 minutes or until brown and bubbly.

Corn Pudding

Serve with a hearty beef dish such as beef burgundy or pot roast. Also good with pork.

Serves 8

1 (15-ounce) can whole kernel corn, drained
1 (14-ounce) can cream-style corn
1 cup milk or half-and-half
¹/4 cup (¹/2 stick) butter, melted

2 eggs, beaten
¹/2 teaspoon salt
¹/4 teaspoon pepper
¹/2 cup cornmeal

*P*reheat the oven to 350 degrees. Combine the whole kernel corn, cream-style corn, milk, butter, eggs, salt and pepper in a bowl and mix well. Stir in the cornmeal.

Spoon the corn mixture into a buttered 2-quart baking dish. Bake for 50 to 55 minutes or until light brown on top and set in the middle. Let stand for 5 minutes before serving.

Broiled Baby Zucchini Boats with Parmesan Crust

Allow the children to sprinkle the cheese over the zucchini, and this may actually entice them to eat the final result.

Serves 4 to 6

1 tablespoon butter	Salt and pepper to taste
2 teaspoons minced garlic	Grated Parmesan cheese
4 small zucchini, cut	to taste
lengthwise into halves	

*H*eat the butter in a large cast-iron skillet or ovenproof skillet. Sauté the garlic in the butter over medium-low heat for 30 seconds; do not brown. Arrange the zucchini cut side down over the garlic butter and sprinkle lightly with salt and pepper.

Sauté over medium heat for 5 minutes or just until slightly tender when pierced with a fork. Turn and sprinkle generously with cheese. Do not be concerned if the cheese spills into the skillet as it will melt into additional delicious crust. Cook for 1 to 2 minutes longer. Preheat the broiler. Broil for 3 to 5 minutes or until brown and bubbly. Serve immediately, scraping the crusty cheese crust from the bottom of the skillet over the zucchini.

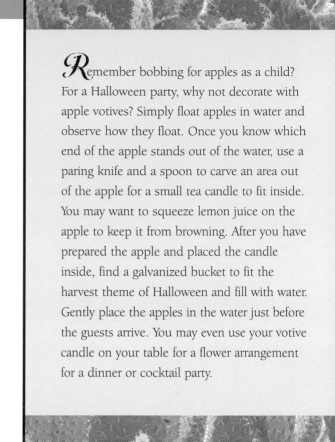

*R*emember bobbing for apples as a child? For a Halloween party, why not decorate with apple votives? Simply float apples in water and observe how they float. Once you know which end of the apple stands out of the water, use a paring knife and a spoon to carve an area out of the apple for a small tea candle to fit inside. You may want to squeeze lemon juice on the apple to keep it from browning. After you have prepared the apple and placed the candle inside, find a galvanized bucket to fit the harvest theme of Halloween and fill with water. Gently place the apples in the water just before the guests arrive. You may even use your votive candle on your table for a flower arrangement for a dinner or cocktail party.

Plentiful Potatoes

Serves 8

1 (2-pound) package frozen hash brown potatoes, thawed	10 ounces Cheddar cheese, shredded
2 cups sour cream or lite sour cream	Salt and pepper to taste
1 (10-ounce) can cream of potato soup	2 cups crushed cornflakes
	1/4 cup (1/2 stick) butter, melted

*P*reheat the oven to 350 degrees. Combine the hash brown potatoes, sour cream, soup, cheese, salt and pepper in a bowl and mix well. Spoon the potato mixture into a shallow baking dish. Toss the cornflakes and butter in a bowl until coated and sprinkle over the prepared layer. Bake for 1 hour.

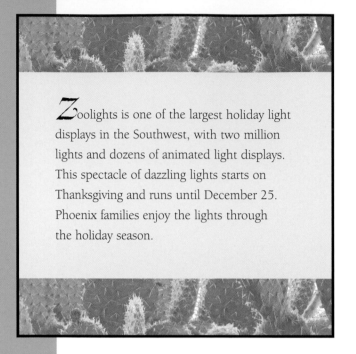

Messy Georges

Serves 6

1 1/2 pounds ground turkey or beef	1 tablespoon yellow mustard
1/2 cup chopped onion	1 tablespoon balsamic vinegar
2 garlic cloves, minced	1 teaspoon sugar
1 (28-ounce) can crushed tomatoes	1 teaspoon chili powder
1 tablespoon tomato paste	1 teaspoon oregano
1 tablespoon soy sauce	1 teaspoon coriander
1 tablespoon Worcestershire sauce	1/2 teaspoon cumin
	1/2 teaspoon pepper
	1/8 teaspoon salt
	6 hamburger buns

Brown the ground turkey in a large nonstick skillet, stirring until crumbly. Drain and spoon into a bowl. Sauté the onion and garlic in the same skillet over medium-high heat for 3 minutes or until the onion is tender. Stir in the undrained tomatoes, tomato paste, soy sauce, Worcestershire sauce, mustard and vinegar. Add the sugar, chili powder, oregano, coriander, cumin, pepper and salt and mix well. Bring to a boil; reduce the heat. Simmer for 20 minutes or until slightly thickened, stirring occasionally. Return the ground turkey to the skillet and mix well. Simmer just until heated through, stirring frequently. Serve on the buns.

Barbecue Cups

Makes 20 cups

1 1/2 pounds ground beef	2 tablespoons dried onion flakes
3/4 cup barbecue sauce	2 (10-count) cans refrigerator biscuits
3 tablespoons brown sugar	3/4 cup (3 ounces) shredded Cheddar cheese

Preheat the oven to 400 degrees. Brown the ground beef in a skillet, stirring until crumbly; drain. Mix in the barbecue sauce, brown sugar and onion flakes and cook just until heated through, stirring frequently. Separate the biscuits and pat each biscuit over the bottom and up the side of an ungreased muffin cup. Spoon the ground beef mixture into the prepared muffin cups and sprinkle with the cheese. Bake for 10 to 12 minutes or until brown and bubbly.

All-in-One Dinosaur Dinner

Very simple and nutritious, and children love to help make it and eat it. Limited cooking skills are needed, but imagination is required.

Serves a crowd

2 pounds unpeeled russet potatoes, cut into chunks
6 tablespoons milk
3 to 5 tablespoons butter, softened
Salt and pepper to taste
Chicken dinosaurs
Broccoli florets, cooked al dente if desired
Whole kernel corn
Shredded purple cabbage
Canned beans
Ketchup, pasta sauce, barbecue sauce or salsa
Shredded cheese

*C*ombine the potatoes with enough water to cover in a saucepan. Bring to a boil and boil until tender; drain. Reserve several potato chunks for the landscape. Return the remaining potatoes to the saucepan and add the milk and butter. Mash until smooth and season with salt and pepper. Let stand until cool. Cook the chicken dinosaurs using the package directions.

Spread the potatoes 1/2 inch thick in a roasting pan or on a baking sheet with sides, mounding some of the potatoes in the shape of a volcano about 6 to 8 inches high. Be sure to create a crater in the top of the volcano, with part of the crater indented for the lava to flow out.

Position the top oven rack far enough from the heat source so that the volcano is close to but does not touch the heating element. Preheat the broiler. Arrange the chicken dinosaurs on the mashed potato layer and create a forest using broccoli florets. Arrange the kernels of corn as a field of flowers and create a stream with the cabbage. The beans can serve as rocks along the stream's edge or volcano. Arrange the reserved potato chunks as rocks to form an outcropping or pile.

Fill the crater with ketchup, allowing to flow down the side, and sprinkle with cheese. Broil until the cheese melts. Set the masterpiece in the center of the table and let everyone enjoy your creation. You may substitute any of the vegetables mentioned with vegetables that your children like or vegetables they do not like but that will add color.

Stromboli with Honey Mustard Dipping Sauce

Serves 4

1 (10-ounce) can refrigerator pizza dough
1/4 teaspoon basil
5 ounces thinly sliced ham, pepperoni or
   meat of choice

2 cups (8 ounces) shredded mozzarella cheese
1 egg, beaten
1 garlic clove, minced
Honey mustard sauce

*P*reheat the oven to 350 degrees. Roll the pizza dough on a hard surface and sprinkle with the basil. Layer with the ham and cheese to within 1/4 inch of the edge. Roll as for a jelly roll and arrange seam side down on a greased baking sheet.

Mix the egg and garlic in a bowl and brush over the top of the roll. Bake for 35 to 40 minutes or until golden brown. Remove to a wire rack to cool. Cut into 11/2-inch slices and serve with honey mustard sauce.

Apple Dumplings

Makes 16 dumplings

2 Granny Smith apples, peeled and each
   cut into 8 slices
2 (8-count) cans crescent rolls
1 cup (2 sticks) butter

2 cups sugar
1/8 teaspoon cinnamon
1 (10-ounce) can Mountain Dew

*P*lace the apples in a microwave-safe dish and microwave for 1 minute. Unroll the roll dough and separate into triangles. Roll each apple slice in a triangle and arrange seam side down in a 9×13-inch baking dish.

Heat the butter in a saucepan until melted and stir in the sugar and cinnamon. Spoon the butter mixture over the prepared layer. Pour the soda around the edges of the dish. Bake for 30 to 40 minutes or until brown. Serve warm with ice cream.

Popcorn Cake

Serves 16

2 teaspoons vegetable oil
12 cups popped plain unsalted unbuttered popcorn
2 cups "M & M's" Plain Chocolate Candies
1/2 cup unsalted cocktail peanuts
1/2 cup salted cocktail peanuts
1/2 cup (1 stick) unsalted butter
1/4 cup vegetable oil
1 (16-ounce) package marshmallows

Coat a large tube pan or bundt pan with 2 teaspoons oil. Toss the popcorn, chocolate candies and peanuts in a bowl until combined. Heat the butter, 1/4 cup oil and marshmallows in a saucepan over medium-low heat until blended, stirring frequently. Pour the marshmallow mixture over the popcorn mixture and stir until coated.

Spoon the popcorn mixture into the prepared pan and press lightly. Let stand, covered with foil, for 3 to 4 hours. Invert onto a cake platter, shaking lightly to release. Serve at room temperature. You may substitute the dulce de leche flavor or the "M & M's" Almond Chocolate Candies for the "M & M's" Chocolate Candies.

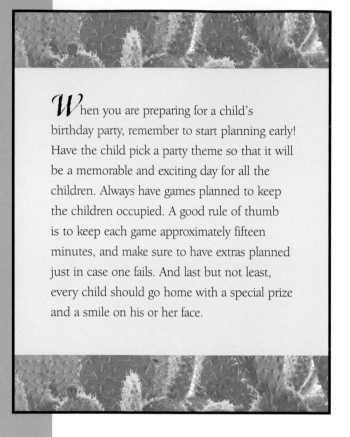

When you are preparing for a child's birthday party, remember to start planning early! Have the child pick a party theme so that it will be a memorable and exciting day for all the children. Always have games planned to keep the children occupied. A good rule of thumb is to keep each game approximately fifteen minutes, and make sure to have extras planned just in case one fails. And last but not least, every child should go home with a special prize and a smile on his or her face.

Chocolate Sheet Cake

Serves 10 to 12

Cake
2 cups sugar
2 cups flour
1 teaspoon baking soda
1/2 teaspoon salt
1 cup water
1/4 cup baking cocoa
2 tablespoons butter
1/2 cup sour cream
2 eggs, lightly beaten

Chocolate Frosting
6 tablespoons milk
1/4 cup baking cocoa
1 tablespoon unsalted butter
1 (1-pound) package confectioners' sugar
1 teaspoon vanilla extract

For the cake, preheat the oven to 350 degrees. Mix the sugar, flour, baking soda and salt in a heatproof bowl. Combine the water, baking cocoa and butter in a small saucepan. Bring to a boil and immediately whisk into the sugar mixture. Stir in the sour cream and eggs. Pour the batter into a 10×15-inch cake pan. Bake for 20 to 25 minutes or until the cake tests done.

For the frosting, bring the milk, baking cocoa and butter to a boil in a saucepan, stirring occasionally. Combine the hot milk mixture, confectioners' sugar and vanilla in a heatproof mixing bowl and beat until smooth; the frosting will be thin. Pour over the cake and let stand until set.

Toffee Crunch Candy

Serves 12 to 15

40 saltine crackers
1 cup (2 sticks) butter, cut into chunks
1 cup packed light brown sugar
2 cups (12 ounces) milk chocolate chips
1 1/2 cups chopped pecans

*P*reheat the oven to 400 degrees. Line a baking sheet with foil and coat with butter. Arrange the crackers salt side up in a single layer on the prepared baking sheet.

Bring 1 cup butter and the brown sugar to a boil in a saucepan over medium-high heat and boil for 3 minutes, stirring frequently. Pour the hot brown sugar mixture over the crackers.

Bake for 5 minutes and remove from the oven. Immediately sprinkle with the chocolate chips. Let stand until the chocolate chips soften and spread evenly over the top. Sprinkle with the pecans. Chill for 1 hour and break into pieces.

Everything Cookies

Makes 2 dozen cookies

1 (18-ounce) roll refrigerator sugar cookie dough, softened
1/2 cup (3 ounces) semisweet chocolate chips
1/2 cup rolled oats
1/2 cup "M & M's" Plain Chocolate Candies
1/3 cup creamy peanut butter
1/3 cup chopped nuts (optional)

*P*reheat the oven to 375 degrees. Unwrap the cookie dough and place in a mixing bowl. Add the chocolate chips, oats, chocolate candies, peanut butter and nuts and mix well.

Drop the dough by spoonfuls 1 inch apart onto a cookie sheet. Bake for 16 to 18 minutes or until light brown. Cool on the cookie sheet for 1 minute. Remove to a wire rack to cool completely and store in an airtight container.

Peanut Butter Marshmallow Treats

Great treat for children and adults of all ages.

Makes 2 dozen treats

3 cups crisp rice cereal
1 cup miniature marshmallows
3/4 cup golden raisins
1/4 cup peanuts, chopped

1/2 cup sugar
1/2 cup light corn syrup
1/2 teaspoon vanilla extract
1/2 cup chunky peanut butter

*T*oss the cereal, marshmallows, raisins and peanuts in a bowl. Bring the sugar, corn syrup and vanilla to a boil in a saucepan over medium heat, stirring constantly. Remove from the heat and stir in the peanut butter until blended. Add the peanut butter mixture to the cereal mixture and stir until coated. Press the cereal mixture over the bottom of an 8×8-inch baking pan sprayed with nonstick cooking spray. Let stand until cool. Cut into squares using a knife coated with nonstick cooking spray.

Patriotic Popsicles

Serve these red, white, and blue popsicles on the Fourth of July.

Makes 8 popsicles

1 1/2 cups frozen red raspberries
1/4 cup sugar, or to taste
1/4 cup water
1/4 cup lemon juice
2 ripe bananas

2 tablespoons sugar, or to taste
1 1/2 cups frozen blueberries
1/4 cup vanilla yogurt
2 tablespoons sugar, or to taste

*P*urée the frozen raspberries, 1/4 cup sugar, water and 1 tablespoon of the lemon juice in a blender. Fill 8 popsicle molds 1/3 full. Insert a popsicle stick into each mold and freeze for 30 minutes or until firm. Check after 10 minutes and reposition any sticks that have fallen over or are not centered.

Process the bananas, 2 tablespoons sugar and 1 tablespoon of the remaining lemon juice in a blender until puréed. Pour the banana mixture over the frozen layer, filling the mold 2/3 full. Freeze for 30 minutes or until firm.

Process the frozen blueberries, yogurt, 2 tablespoons sugar and the remaining lemon juice in a blender until puréed. Pour over the frozen layers, filling to the top of the mold. Freeze for 2 hours or until firm.

Cinnamon Pull

Include this pastry on your Christmas morning buffet.

Serves 12 to 14

1/2 cup coarsely chopped walnuts
1/2 cup sugar
1 tablespoon cinnamon
1 cup packed brown sugar
1/2 cup (1 stick) butter
8 ounces cream cheese
2 (10-count) cans refrigerator biscuits

*P*reheat the oven to 350 degrees. Spray a bundt pan with nonstick cooking spray and sprinkle 1/3 of the walnuts over the bottom of the pan. Mix the sugar and cinnamon in a bowl. Combine the brown sugar and butter in a saucepan and cook over low heat until blended, stirring frequently.

Cut the cream cheese into 20 equal cubes. Pat the biscuits into thin rounds and sprinkle each round with 1/2 teaspoon of the sugar and cinnamon mixture. Place 1 cream cheese cube in the center of each round and wrap and seal the dough to enclose the filling. Arrange 1/2 of the cream cheese-stuffed biscuits in the prepared pan. Sprinkle with 1/2 of the remaining cinnamon and sugar mixture, drizzle with 1/2 of the butter mixture and sprinkle with 1/2 of the remaining walnuts. Layer the prepared layers with the remaining cream cheese-stuffed biscuits, remaining cinnamon and sugar mixture, remaining butter mixture and remaining walnuts. Bake for 50 minutes. Let stand for 5 minutes and invert onto a serving plate.

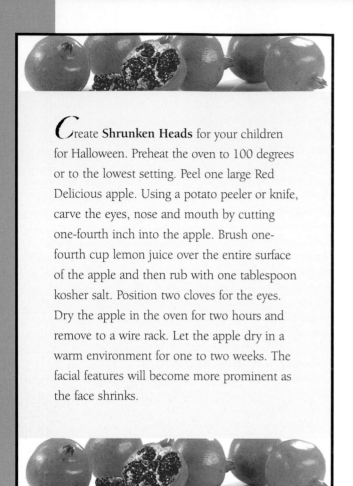

Create **Shrunken Heads** for your children for Halloween. Preheat the oven to 100 degrees or to the lowest setting. Peel one large Red Delicious apple. Using a potato peeler or knife, carve the eyes, nose and mouth by cutting one-fourth inch into the apple. Brush one-fourth cup lemon juice over the entire surface of the apple and then rub with one tablespoon kosher salt. Position two cloves for the eyes. Dry the apple in the oven for two hours and remove to a wire rack. Let the apple dry in a warm environment for one to two weeks. The facial features will become more prominent as the face shrinks.

Pumpkin Roll

This will be a great hit at Thanksgiving.

Serves 8 to 10

Cake
3/4 cup flour
2 teaspoons cinnamon
1 teaspoon each nutmeg,
   ginger and baking powder
1/2 teaspoon salt
1 cup sugar
3 eggs, lightly beaten
2/3 cup canned pumpkin
1 cup chopped pecans
Confectioners' sugar

Cream Cheese Filling and Assembly
8 ounces cream
   cheese, softened
1 cup confectioners' sugar
3 tablespoons butter, softened
1 teaspoon vanilla extract
Walnut halves

For the cake, preheat the oven to 375 degrees. Grease a 10×15-inch jelly roll pan and line with waxed paper. Grease and flour the waxed paper. Sift 3/4 cup flour, the cinnamon, nutmeg, ginger, baking powder and salt together. Beat the sugar and eggs in a mixing bowl until thickened and fluffy. Add the pumpkin and beat until smooth. Stir in the flour mixture until blended.

Pour the batter into the prepared pan and spread evenly with a rubber spatula. Sprinkle with the pecans. Bake for 15 minutes. Run a sharp knife around the edges of the cake to loosen and invert onto a clean tea towel dusted with confectioners' sugar. Remove the waxed paper and roll the warm cake in the towel as for a jelly roll from the short side. Cool on a wire rack for 45 minutes.

For the filling, beat the cream cheese, confectioners' sugar, butter and vanilla in a mixing bowl until blended, scraping the bowl occasionally.

To serve, unroll the cake roll carefully and remove the towel. Spread the filling to within 1 inch of the edge and roll as for a jelly roll to enclose the filling. Garnish with walnut halves. Serve immediately or wrap in plastic wrap and store in the refrigerator. Let stand at room temperature for 15 to 30 minutes before slicing.

Cream Cheese Cookies with Royal Icing

Children young and old will delight in having these cookies for Easter dinner.

Makes 3 dozen large cookies, or 4 dozen medium cookies

Cookies
8 ounces cream cheese, softened
1 cup (2 sticks) butter, softened
2 cups sugar
1 egg
1 teaspoon each almond and vanilla extract
3^1/$_2$ cups flour
1 teaspoon baking powder

Royal Icing
1 (1-pound) package confectioners' sugar
3 tablespoons meringue powder
3 to 5 tablespoons warm water
Food coloring

*F*or the cookies, beat the cream cheese and butter in a mixing bowl until creamy, scraping the bowl occasionally. Add the sugar, egg and flavorings and beat until blended. Beat in ^{1}/$_2$ cup of the flour and the baking powder until smooth. Add the remaining 3 cups flour 1 cup at a time, beating well after each addition and scraping the bowl frequently. Divide the dough into 2 equal portions and place each portion on a sheet of plastic wrap. Pat each portion into a flat disc and wrap with the plastic wrap. Chill for 3 to 10 hours.

Preheat the oven to 375 degrees. Remove 1 of the chilled dough portions from the refrigerator and roll ^{1}/$_8$ to ^{1}/$_4$ inch thick on a lightly floured surface with a floured rolling pin. If making a cookie bouquet, a ^{1}/$_4$-inch thickness is preferred. Cut into desired shapes with cookie cutters. Arrange 1 to 2 inches apart on an ungreased cookie sheet. For cookie bouquets, insert the sticks when placed on the cookie sheet. Squeeze a bit of the dough around the insertion point to keep the sticks in place when removed from the oven. When decorating, add a little of the icing to the insertion point. Bake for 8 to 12 minutes or until the edges are firm and light brown. Cool on the cookie sheet for 5 to 6 minutes and remove to a wire rack to cool completely. Repeat the process with the remaining dough portion.

For the icing, sift the confectioners' sugar into a mixing bowl fitted with a whisk attachment. Add the meringue powder and mix until blended. Add the water 1 tablespoon at a time, mixing constantly at low speed until it adheres. Continue beating at medium to high speed for 3 minutes; do not overbeat. Blend in desired food coloring. Use this consistency for outlining the cookies or adding interest to already frosted cookies.

To make a spreadable icing, spoon about 1 cup of the icing into a small bowl. Add water 1 teaspoon or less at a time until the icing flows easily when stirred but still has a little body. If the consistency is too thin, add confectioners' sugar 1 teaspoon at a time until thickened. Always cover the icing well with plastic wrap to keep it from crusting. Once crusted, the icing is virtually impossible to get smooth again, which means it is unusable.

Hot air balloons dot the horizon morning and evening throughout the Valley of the Sun. Their colorful designs seem to stand still as they travel across the desert floor making a special day well remembered. If you'd rather keep your feet on the ground, enjoy a spring afternoon picnicking under the sun in one of Phoenix's many neighborhood parks. Art, chocolate, and other culinary festivals are held in many cities in the metropolitan area and are an enjoyable way to spend a casual afternoon. End the evening as you catch a glimpse of the most amazing sunsets in the world. Romantic and awe-inspiring, these sunsets provide the perfect backdrop for a cozy dinner for two.

Just the Two of You

Cocktails
Frozen Peach Champagne Cocktail
Chocolate Martini

Appetizers
Smoked Alaskan Salmon Bruschetta
Feta Olive Spread
Apricot Baked Brie
Baked Smoked Gouda
Grilled Tandoori-Style Shrimp with Mint Chutney

Sides
Braised Leeks
Mushrooms with Garlic Butter and Pine Nuts
Goat Cheese Mashed Potatoes
Spinach Gratin

Main Courses
Stuffed Beef Tenderloin with
       Merlot Peppercorn Sauce
Rack of Lamb with Mustard Thyme Crust
Roast Pork Tenderloin with Plum Sauce
Classic Coq au Vin
Roasted King Salmon with
       Pinot Noir Mustard Sauce
Pan-Seared Scallops with Beurre Blanc Sauce
Penne with Butternut Squash and Sage
Spaghetti Bolognese

Desserts
Moist Lemon Cups
Strawberries Romanoff
Molten Chocolate Cake
Coconut Cream Pie

Just the
Two of You

recipes for romancing

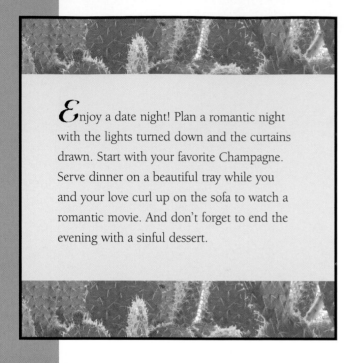

Frozen Peach Champagne Cocktail

Serves 4

1/4 cup sugar
1 pint peach sorbet
2 shots Triple Sec, Grand Marnier or Cointreau
Champagne or sparkling wine, chilled
Fresh raspberries
4 sprigs of mint

*P*our the sugar into a shallow dish. Moisten the rims of 4 cocktail glasses with water and dip the rims in the sugar, rotating gently to cover evenly. Combine the sorbet and liqueur in a blender and add Champagne to the maximum fill line. Process until smooth and pour into the prepared glasses. Garnish each with fresh raspberries and a sprig of mint. Serve immediately.

Chocolate Martini

Serves 8 to 10

2 1/2 cups vodka
1 1/4 cups chocolate liqueur
1/4 cup raspberry liqueur (Chambord)

Ghirardelli milk chocolate chips, melted
Ghirardelli sweet ground chocolate

*M*ix the vodka, chocolate liqueur and raspberry liqueur in a pitcher and chill for 1 to 2 hours. Dip the rims of 8 to 10 chilled martini glasses in melted chocolate chips and immediately dust with ground chocolate. Let stand until dry. Pour the chilled martinis into the chocolate-rimmed glasses and serve immediately.

Smoked Alaskan Salmon Bruschetta

Serves 4

$1/2$ cup chopped ripe tomato
$1/4$ cup julienned fresh basil
2 tablespoons feta cheese
$1/4$ cup flaked smoked Alaskan king salmon, lox or other smoked fish
12 diagonally cut ($1/2$-inch) slices baguette
$1/4$ cup extra-virgin olive oil

*P*reheat the oven to 400 degrees. Combine the tomatoes, basil, cheese and salmon in a bowl and mix well. Brush both sides of the bread slices with the olive oil or rub with fresh garlic.

Arrange the slices in a single layer on a baking sheet and toast until brown and crisp. Remove from the oven and cool to room temperature. Top each slice with some of the salmon mixture.

Feta Olive Spread

Serves 10 to 12

4 ounces cream cheese, softened
4 ounces feta cheese
2 tablespoons lemon juice
$1/2$ teaspoon oregano
1 garlic clove, chopped
$1/2$ (16-ounce) can pitted olives, drained

*C*ombine the cream cheese, feta cheese, lemon juice, oregano and garlic in a food processor and process until smooth. Add the olives and pulse until the olives are chopped and combined. Serve with assorted party crackers or party bread.

For **Cheese Bruschetta**, spread the feta mixture on toasted baguette slices and sprinkle with chopped fresh herbs.

Apricot Baked Brie

Serves 6

Candied Pecans
1 cup pecans
1/2 cup sugar

Brie
2 shallots, finely chopped
1 tablespoon butter
1/2 cup apricot preserves
1 (7-ounce) round Brie cheese

*F*or the pecans, combine the pecans and sugar in a skillet. Cook over medium heat for 5 minutes or until the sugar melts and the pecans are coated, shaking the pan frequently. Spread the pecan mixture on a sheet of foil and let stand until cool. Break into small pieces.

For the Brie, preheat the oven to 350 degrees. Sauté the shallots in the butter in a small skillet until tender. Combine the sautéed shallots, candied pecans and preserves in a bowl and mix well.

Place the Brie round on a baking sheet and spread the preserves mixture over the top of the Brie. Bake for 10 minutes. Serve with assorted party crackers.

Baked Smoked Gouda

Serves 4 to 6

1 round smoked Gouda cheese, about 2 inches thick
1 (8-count) can crescent rolls

*P*reheat the oven using the roll package directions. Cut the Gouda horizontally into 2 equal halves. Unroll the roll dough and separate into 4 rectangles. Place 1 cheese half in the center of 1 rectangle and position another rectangle in the opposite direction over the cheese. Pinch the edges to seal and place on a baking sheet. Repeat the process with the remaining cheese and remaining roll dough.

Bake using the roll package directions until the cheese is soft but not runny. Cut each into halves and then into strips. Serve with baguette slices and a glass of red or white wine.

Grilled Tandoori-Style Shrimp with Mint Chutney

Serves 4

1¹/2 pounds jumbo (16- to 20-count) shrimp, peeled
1 teaspoon turmeric
1 teaspoon paprika
¹/2 teaspoon kosher salt
¹/4 teaspoon pepper
Mint Chutney (sidebar)

*C*oat the grill rack with oil and position the rack 5 to 6 inches from the heat source. Preheat the grill. Butterfly the shrimp by making a lengthwise slit to but not through the other side, starting from the top to the bottom down the center of the back; devein. Combine the turmeric, paprika, salt and pepper in a bowl and mix well. Add the shrimp to the turmeric mixture and toss to coat.

Arrange the shrimp opened flat on the grill rack and grill for 2 minutes per side or until cooked through, turning once. Serve with the Mint Chutney. You may grill the shrimp in an oiled ridged grill pan over medium heat.

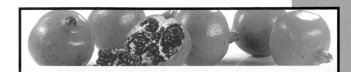

*S*erve **Mint Chutney** with Grilled Tandoori-Style Shrimp. Sauté ¹/2 cup chopped onion in 1 tablespoon olive oil in a small skillet over medium heat until light brown. Stir in ¹/4 cup coarsely chopped golden raisins, ¹/4 cup water, 3 tablespoons white wine vinegar, ¹/4 teaspoon hot red pepper flakes, ¹/4 teaspoon coriander and ¹/4 teaspoon salt. Simmer for 2 minutes, stirring frequently. Spoon the chutney into a bowl and let stand until cool. Stir in ¹/2 cup chopped fresh mint.

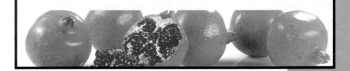

Stuffed Beef Tenderloin with Merlot Peppercorn Sauce

Serves 6 to 8

Beef Tenderloin

1 (2½- to 3-pound) beef tenderloin
¼ cup (½ stick) unsalted butter
4 garlic cloves, minced
3 cups chopped frozen spinach, thawed
   and drained
1 egg, beaten
1¾ cups seasoned bread crumbs
1 teaspoon nutmeg
Salt and pepper to taste

Merlot Peppercorn Sauce

½ cup merlot
1 shallot, minced
2 tablespoons coarsely crushed
   four-peppercorn mix
1¾ cups chicken stock
1¾ cups beef stock
¼ cup (½ stick) butter, softened
¼ cup milk
1 tablespoon cornstarch

*F*or the tenderloin, preheat the oven to 375 degrees. Have the butcher butterfly the tenderloin and pound into an 8×14-inch rectangle. Mix the butter and garlic in a bowl and spread over the cut surface of the tenderloin. Press the excess moisture from the spinach and mix with the egg, bread crumbs and nutmeg in a bowl. Spread the spinach mixture over the butter mixture and roll the tenderloin, beginning from the long side, to enclose the filling. Secure with kitchen twine and arrange seam side down in a roasting pan. You may prepare to this point up to 1 day in advance and store, covered, in the refrigerator. Bring to room temperature before proceeding with the recipe.

Sprinkle salt and pepper over the surface of the tenderloin and insert a meat thermometer. Roast for 35 minutes or until the meat thermometer registers 145 degrees for medium-rare. Tent with foil and let stand for 15 minutes. Slice as desired.

For the sauce, bring the wine, shallot and peppercorns to a boil in a saucepan; reduce the heat. Simmer for 5 minutes or until the mixture is reduced by ½, stirring frequently. Stir in the chicken stock and beef stock and bring to a boil. Boil for 25 minutes or until the mixture is reduced to 2 cups, stirring occasionally. Stir in the butter and milk. Sift the cornstarch into the mixture, whisking constantly.

Cook for 4 minutes or until the sauce coats the back of a spoon, stirring frequently. Serve with the tenderloin. The sauce may be prepared up to 2 hours in advance. Let stand, covered, at room temperature. Reheat before serving.

Rack of Lamb with Mustard Thyme Crust

Serves 2

1 (1¹/4-pound) rack of lamb, trimmed
Salt and pepper to taste
¹/3 cup Dijon mustard
1 tablespoon chopped fresh thyme, or
   1 teaspoon dried thyme

1 tablespoon minced garlic
1 cup fresh French bread crumbs
2 tablespoons olive oil
Sprigs of fresh thyme (optional)

*P*reheat the oven to 425 degrees. Arrange the lamb round side up on a baking sheet with sides and sprinkle with salt and pepper. Whisk the mustard, chopped thyme and garlic in a bowl and spread evenly over the surface of the lamb. You may prepare to this point up to 6 hours in advance and store, uncovered, in the refrigerator.

Sauté the bread crumbs in the olive oil in a heavy skillet over medium heat for 5 minutes or until crisp. Cool slightly. Press the crumbs over the surface of the lamb. Roast for 25 minutes or until a meat thermometer inserted in the center registers 145 degrees for medium-rare. Garnish with sprigs of thyme.

Roast Pork Tenderloin with Plum Sauce

Serves 6

1 pork tenderloin
Onion salt to taste
Garlic salt to taste
Salt and pepper to taste

1 small onion, finely chopped
¹/2 cup (1 stick) butter
1 small jar plum preserves
Soy sauce to taste

*P*reheat the oven to 350 degrees. Season the tenderloin with onion salt, garlic salt, salt and pepper and arrange in a baking pan. Roast, covered with foil, for approximately 1 hour.

Sauté the onion in the butter in a skillet until tender. Stir in the preserves and soy sauce. Cook until of a sauce consistency, stirring frequently. Remove the foil from the tenderloin and brush with the plum sauce. Roast for 30 minutes longer or to the desired degree of doneness, basting with the plum sauce frequently. Slice as desired and serve with hot cooked rice and the remaining plum sauce.

Classic Coq au Vin

Serves 4 to 6

1 pound fresh button mushrooms
10 slices bacon, cut into 1/2-inch pieces
2 chicken breasts
2 chicken thighs
2 chicken legs
1/2 teaspoon salt
1/4 teaspoon freshly ground pepper
1 onion, finely chopped
20 small pearl onions
1/2 cup minced shallots (2 large shallots)

1 head garlic, separated into cloves
1/4 cup flour
2 teaspoons tomato paste
3 cups full-bodied dry red wine, such as pinot
   noir or Cotes du Rhone
1 1/2 cups chicken stock
6 sprigs of fresh thyme, or 1 teaspoon
   dried thyme
1 bay leaf
2 tablespoons chopped fresh parsley

*C*ut the mushrooms into halves or quarters to match the size of the pearl onions. Cook the bacon in a Dutch oven over high heat until the fat is rendered and the bacon is brown and crisp. Remove the bacon with a slotted spoon to a paper towel to drain, reserving the pan drippings.

Preheat the oven to 350 degrees. Sprinkle the chicken with the salt and pepper. Brown the chicken on all sides in the reserved pan drippings over high heat. Remove the chicken to a platter, reserving 1/4 cup of the pan drippings; reduce the heat to medium-high.

Cook the chopped onion, pearl onions, shallots and garlic cloves in the reserved pan drippings for 4 minutes or until the onions and shallots are tender, stirring frequently. Stir in the mushrooms and cook for 5 minutes longer or until the mushrooms have released most of their moisture and have begun to brown, stirring frequently. Stir in the flour and tomato paste.

Cook for 1 minute, stirring constantly. Add the wine and stock gradually, stirring constantly. Add the bacon, chicken, thyme and bay leaf and mix well. Bring to a boil, stirring occasionally. Bake, covered, for 1 1/2 hours or until the chicken is cooked through.

Remove the chicken with a slotted spoon to a platter and cover loosely to keep warm, reserving the pan juices. Skim the fat from the surface of the juices and cook over medium-high heat for 15 to 20 minutes or until the sauce is slightly thickened and coats the back of a spoon, stirring frequently. Discard the bay leaf and taste and adjust the seasonings. Return the chicken to the Dutch oven and turn to coat. Cook just until heated through, stirring occasionally, and sprinkle with the parsley. Serve with hot cooked egg noodles and Braised Leeks on page 182. You may prepare 1 to 2 days in advance and store, covered, in the refrigerator. Reheat over low heat before serving.

Roasted King Salmon with Pinot Noir Mustard Sauce

Serves 6

Pinot Noir Mustard Sauce

1 cup pinot noir or other red wine
1/4 cup honey
1/4 cup black mustard seeds
1/2 cup red wine vinegar
2 teaspoons chopped fresh tarragon
1 teaspoon chopped shallot
1/2 teaspoon salt
Freshly ground pepper to taste

Salmon and Assembly

6 (6-ounce) fresh King salmon steaks or fillets
Salt and pepper to taste
2 tablespoons olive oil or melted butter
1 bunch fresh arugula, trimmed
1 red bell pepper, chopped

For the sauce, boil the wine in a nonreactive saucepan over high heat until reduced by 1/2. Remove from the heat and add the honey, stirring until the honey dissolves.

Heat the mustard seeds in a dry skillet until they begin to pop and release their aroma. Remove from the heat and stir into the honey mixture. Stir in the vinegar, tarragon, shallot, salt and pepper. Pour the sauce into a jar with a tight-fitting lid and chill in the refrigerator for 8 to 10 hours. You may prepare up to 1 week in advance.

For the salmon, preheat the oven to 450 degrees. Arrange the salmon in a greased baking pan and sprinkle with salt and pepper. Brush both sides with the olive oil. Roast for 5 to 10 minutes or to the desired degree of doneness.

To serve, reheat the sauce if desired or bring to room temperature. Divide the arugula evenly among 6 serving plates and drizzle each serving with 1 tablespoon of the sauce. Arrange 1 salmon steak on each plate. Drizzle each serving with 1 tablespoon of the remaining sauce and sprinkle evenly with the bell pepper. Serve immediately.

Pan-Seared Scallops with Beurre Blanc Sauce

Serves 4

Beurre Blanc Sauce

3/4 cup water
6 tablespoons white wine vinegar
1/4 cup finely chopped shallots
2 tablespoons heavy cream
10 tablespoons (11/4 sticks) unsalted butter, chilled and cut into tablespoons
1/16 teaspoon ground white pepper
Salt to taste

Scallops

11/4 pounds sea scallops
Salt and white pepper to taste
1/4 cup flour
2 tablespoons olive oil
4 teaspoons chopped fresh chives

*F*or the sauce, bring the water, vinegar and shallots to a boil in a heavy saucepan over medium-high heat. Boil for 10 minutes or until the mixture is reduced to 1/4 cup, stirring occasionally. Stir in the heavy cream and reduce the heat to low. Add the butter 1 tablespoon at a time and cook just until melted after each addition, whisking constantly. Strain the sauce, pressing on the solids to extract as much liquid as possible, and return the sauce to the pan. Season with the white pepper and salt and cover. Place the saucepan in a skillet of warm water.

For the scallops, sprinkle the scallops with salt and white pepper and coat with the flour, shaking off the excess. Heat the olive oil in a large nonstick skillet over medium-high heat. Sear the scallops in the hot oil for 11/2 minutes per side or until golden brown and just opaque in the center. To serve, divide the scallops evenly among 4 serving plates and drizzle with the sauce. Sprinkle with the chives and serve immediately.

Penne with Butternut Squash and Sage

Serves 4

16 ounces penne
3 tablespoons olive oil
5 shallots, minced
1 butternut squash, peeled and chopped
1/16 teaspoon allspice
Salt and pepper to taste
3/4 cup chicken broth
Balsamic vinegar to taste
8 fresh sage leaves, julienned
4 ounces thinly sliced prosciutto, cut into narrow strips
Olive oil to taste
1 cup (4 ounces) grated Parmigiano-Reggiano cheese

Cook the pasta using the package directions. Drain and cover to keep warm. Heat 3 tablespoons olive oil in a saucepan over high heat. Add the shallots to the hot oil and sauté for 3 to 4 minutes or until softened. Add the squash, allspice, salt and pepper and mix well.

Sauté for 2 minutes. Stir in the broth and reduce the heat to medium-low. Simmer, covered, for 8 minutes or until the squash is fork tender; do not stir. Remove from the heat and gently stir in vinegar. Taste and adjust the seasonings.

Spoon the squash mixture over the pasta in a bowl. Add the sage, prosciutto and a drizzle of olive oil and toss gently to mix. Sprinkle with the cheese.

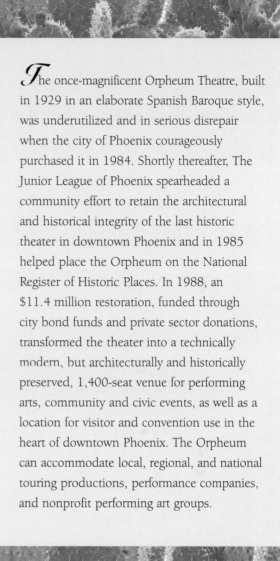

The once-magnificent Orpheum Theatre, built in 1929 in an elaborate Spanish Baroque style, was underutilized and in serious disrepair when the city of Phoenix courageously purchased it in 1984. Shortly thereafter, The Junior League of Phoenix spearheaded a community effort to retain the architectural and historical integrity of the last historic theater in downtown Phoenix and in 1985 helped place the Orpheum on the National Register of Historic Places. In 1988, an $11.4 million restoration, funded through city bond funds and private sector donations, transformed the theater into a technically modern, but architecturally and historically preserved, 1,400-seat venue for performing arts, community and civic events, as well as a location for visitor and convention use in the heart of downtown Phoenix. The Orpheum can accommodate local, regional, and national touring productions, performance companies, and nonprofit performing art groups.

Spaghetti Bolognese

Serves 6

1 (28-ounce) can Italian whole tomatoes
10 ounces pancetta or bacon, chopped
1 cup finely chopped carrots
1 cup finely chopped onion
3/4 cup finely chopped celery
12 ounces ground chuck
8 ounces ground veal
1/2 cup chicken livers, chopped
Salt and pepper to taste
1/2 cup dry white wine
1 tablespoon minced garlic
1 tablespoon Italian tomato paste
1/4 cup heavy cream
16 ounces spaghetti, cooked and drained
Freshly grated Parmesan cheese
1/4 cup chopped Italian parsley

*C*hop the tomatoes, reserving the tomatoes and juice. Cook the pancetta in a saucepan over medium heat for 8 minutes or until most of the fat is rendered, stirring frequently Stir in the carrots, onion and celery and sauté for 3 minutes or until the vegetables are tender.

Combine the ground chuck, ground veal and chicken livers in a bowl and mix well. Season with salt and pepper. Add the ground chuck mixture to the vegetable mixture and mix well. Increase the heat to high and cook for 5 minutes or until the ground chuck mixture is brown, stirring frequently. Stir in the wine, garlic, tomato paste, reserved tomatoes and reserved juice.

Cook, partially covered, over low heat for 2 hours, stirring occasionally and adding additional liquid as needed for the desired consistency. Stir in the heavy cream and season with salt and pepper. Spoon the sauce over the pasta on a serving platter and sprinkle with cheese and the parsley.

Moist Lemon Cups

Serves 4

$1/2$ cup sugar

2 tablespoons flour

2 teaspoons snipped fresh thyme, or $1/2$ teaspoon dried thyme

1 teaspoon finely shredded lemon zest

$1/8$ teaspoon salt

2 egg yolks, lightly beaten

3 tablespoons lemon juice

1 tablespoon butter, melted

$3/4$ cup milk

2 egg whites

Sprigs of fresh thyme

*P*reheat the oven to 325 degrees. Combine the sugar, flour, snipped thyme, lemon zest and salt in a bowl and mix well. Combine the egg yolks, lemon juice and butter in a bowl and mix until blended. Stir the milk into the egg yolk mixture until blended and stir the egg yolk mixture into the sugar mixture.

Beat the egg whites in a mixing bowl at medium speed until soft peaks form. Beat at high speed until stiff peaks form. Fold the egg whites into the egg mixture; the batter will be thin.

Arrange four 6-ounce custard cups in a 9×9-inch baking pan. Pour the batter evenly into the cups, filling almost to the top. Arrange the baking pan on the oven rack and pour enough hot water into the baking pan to measure 1 inch. Bake for 35 to 40 minutes or until the tops are light brown and puffed. Remove the cups to a wire rack and serve warm, garnished with sprigs of thyme. You may chill, covered, in the refrigerator for up to 24 hours. Invert the chilled custards onto dessert plates and garnish with whipped cream and/or fresh raspberries and sprigs of thyme.

Strawberries Romanoff

Serves 10 to 12

4 ounces seedless raisins
2 tablespoons brandy
2 cups sour cream
4 ounces light brown sugar
$1/2$ teaspoon cinnamon

$1/16$ teaspoon nutmeg
Fresh strawberries, peaches, pears
    or raspberries
Confectioners' sugar to taste

*P*rocess the raisins and brandy in a blender until puréed. Add the sour cream, brown sugar, cinnamon and nutmeg and process until blended.

Spoon the strawberries into individual ramekins or custard cups. Spoon the raisin sauce over the strawberries and dust with confectioners' sugar. Serve immediately.

Molten Chocolate Cake

Serves 4

$1/2$ cup (1 stick) unsalted butter
6 ounces bittersweet chocolate, chopped
2 eggs
2 egg yolks

$1/4$ cup sugar
$1/16$ teaspoon salt
2 tablespoons flour

*P*reheat the oven to 450 degrees. Coat four 6-ounce ramekins with butter and sprinkle with flour, shaking off the excess flour. Heat $1/2$ cup butter and the chocolate in a double boiler over simmering water until blended, stirring frequently. Combine the eggs, egg yolks, sugar and salt in a mixing bowl and beat at high speed until thick and pale yellow in color. Whisk the chocolate mixture until smooth and fold into the egg mixture along with 2 tablespoons flour.

Spoon the batter evenly into the prepared ramekins. Arrange the ramekins on a baking sheet and bake for 12 minutes or until the sides of the cakes are firm but the centers are soft. Cool for 1 minute and run a sharp knife around the edge of each cake. Invert onto a dessert plate and let stand for a few seconds before removing the ramekins. Serve immediately.

Coconut Cream Pie

Serves 6 to 8

Vanilla Wafer Crust
35 vanilla wafers
1/3 cup dry-roasted macadamia nuts
1/3 cup sweetened flaked coconut
1/4 cup (1/2 stick) unsalted butter, melted

Coconut Filling
1/2 cup sugar
3 tablespoons flour
2 eggs, beaten
1 egg yolk, beaten

3/4 cup milk
3/4 cup coconut milk
1 1/2 cups sweetened flaked coconut
1 teaspoon vanilla extract
1/8 teaspoon coconut extract

Topping
2/3 cup sweetened flaked coconut
1 1/4 cups whipping cream, chilled
2 tablespoons sugar
1/8 teaspoon coconut extract

*F*or the crust, process the cookies and macadamia nuts in a food processor until ground. Combine the ground cookie mixture and coconut in a bowl and mix well. Stir in the butter. Press the crumb mixture over the bottom and up the side of a 9-inch pie plate. Freeze, covered, for 30 minutes. You may prepare to this point up to 1 week in advance and store, covered, in the freezer. Preheat the oven to 350 degrees. Bake for 20 minutes or until golden brown. Cool on a wire rack.

For the filling, mix the sugar and flour in a bowl. Add the eggs and egg yolk and whisk until blended. Bring the milk, coconut milk and coconut to a simmer in a medium saucepan over medium heat, stirring occasionally. Add the hot milk mixture to the egg mixture gradually, whisking constantly. Return the milk mixture to the saucepan and cook for 4 minutes or until the mixture thickens and comes to a boil, stirring constantly. Remove from the heat and stir in the flavorings. Spoon the coconut mixture into a bowl and press plastic wrap directly onto the surface. Chill for 2 hours or until cold or for up to 8 hours. Spoon the filling into the prepared crust and chill, covered, for 8 to 10 hours.

For the topping, toast the coconut in a small skillet over medium heat for 3 minutes or until light brown, stirring frequently. Let stand until cool. Beat the whipping cream, sugar and flavoring in a mixing bowl until peaks form. Spread the whipped cream over the top of the filling, sealing to the edge. Sprinkle with the toasted coconut. You may prepare up to 4 hours in advance and store, covered, in the refrigerator. Serve chilled.

Phoenix, also known as the Valley of the Sun, glows nightly throughout the holiday season at The Desert Botanical Gardens, home to the world's largest and most diverse collection of succulent plants. During the holidays, the prickly pear cacti and other plant species are aglow with luminaries, small paper bags illuminated by candles, that line the trails throughout the Gardens. Within walking distance, the Phoenix Zoo presents ZooLights, an annual celebration in which millions of sparkling lights dance in the darkness in the form of favorite zoo animals. The glow of holiday lights creates a festive atmosphere to enjoy special celebrations with family and friends.

Valley Glow

photo donated by The Desert Botanical Gardens
photo © Gene Almendinger

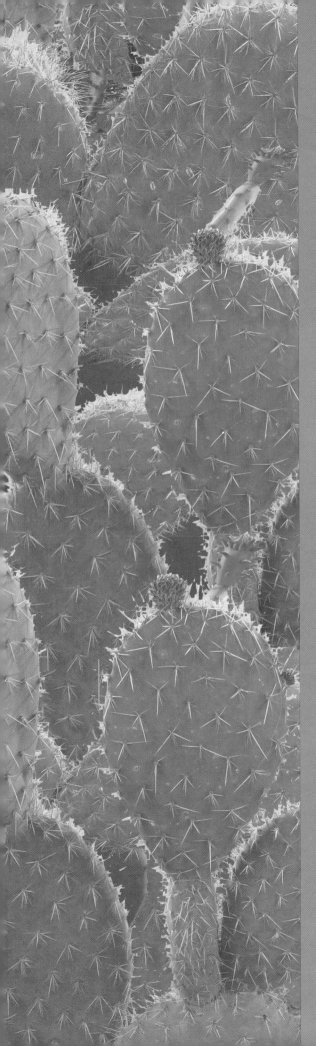

Beverages
Creamy Hot Chocolate
Glögg

Appetizers
Bruschetta with Arugula and
       Rosemary White Bean Spread
Baked Brie with Garlic Fig Compote
Caviar Pie

Soups and Salads
Potage Crécy
Roasted Butternut Squash Soup
Creamy Shellfish Soup
Festive Arugula Salad with Oranges, Pomegranate
       Seeds and Goat Cheese
Jicama Pomegranate Salad

Sides
Baked Apricots
Sautéed Haricots Verts, Red Bell Peppers and
       Pine Nuts
Mushroom and Orzo Pilaf
Twice-Baked Gorgonzola Potatoes
Stuffed Tomatoes
Risotto Milanese

Main Courses
Herbed Beef Tenderloin with Red Wine Sauce
Osso Buco with Gremolata
Pork Tenderloin with Balsamic Cranberry Sauce
Sausage Spinach Wreath with Apple Salsa
Cornish Game Hens with Apple Plum Stuffing

Desserts
Baked Apples with Marsala-Soaked Raisins
Eggnog Ice Cream
Almond Roca
Bourbon Pumpkin Cheesecake
Bacardi Rum Cake

Valley Glow

hors d'oeuvre and holiday party specialties

Creamy Hot Chocolate

Serves 2

1/3 cup whipping cream, chilled
1 tablespoon sugar
4 ounces bittersweet chocolate
2 cups milk

*B*eat the whipping cream in a mixing bowl until soft peaks form. Add the sugar and beat just until stiff peaks form. Chop the chocolate, reserving 2 teaspoons. Heat the remaining chocolate and milk in a small saucepan over medium heat just until the mixture begins to simmer, stirring occasionally. Pour the hot chocolate into 2 large mugs and top with the whipped cream. Sprinkle with the reserved chocolate and serve immediately. For an added treat, add 1 to 2 ounces peppermint schnapps to the hot chocolate.

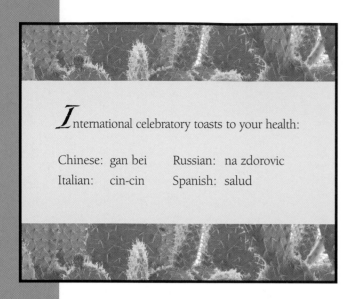

*I*nternational celebratory toasts to your health:

Chinese: gan bei   Russian: na zdorovic
Italian: cin-cin   Spanish: salud

Glögg

Serves 4 to 5

3 cinnamon sticks
1/4 whole nutmeg, grated
10 whole cloves
1/4 teaspoon allspice berries
1 quart red wine
1 cup sugar

3/4 cup aquavit
3/4 cup ruby port
6 tablespoons brandy
Whole blanched almonds
4 to 5 teaspoons wine-soaked raisins

*T*ie the cinnamon sticks, nutmeg, cloves and allspice berries in cheesecloth. Combine the cheesecloth pouch, red wine and sugar in a saucepan. Cook over medium heat until steaming, stirring occasionally. Stir in the aquavit, port and brandy. Heat until steaming; do not boil. Taste and add additional sugar if desired. Discard the cheesecloth pouch.

To serve, place 2 to 3 almonds and 1 teaspoon of soaked raisins in a mug or heatproof glass and fill with the Glögg.

Bruschetta with Arugula and Rosemary White Bean Spread

Serves 6 to 8

1 baguette French bread, sliced
1 (15-ounce) can cannellini beans, drained
   and rinsed
2 tablespoons olive oil
2 tablespoons water
1 tablespoon fresh lemon juice
1 small garlic clove, crushed
$1/2$ teaspoon salt

$1/8$ teaspoon freshly ground pepper
$1/4$ teaspoon chopped fresh rosemary
1 tablespoon olive oil
1 tablespoon balsamic vinegar
$1/4$ teaspoon salt
$1/8$ teaspoon pepper
$1/4$ cup thinly sliced red onion
1 small bunch arugula, trimmed and julienned

*P*reheat the oven to 400 degrees. Arrange the bread slices in a single layer on a baking sheet and toast for 5 to 8 minutes or until light brown. Remove to a wire rack to cool.

Combine $2/3$ of the beans, 2 tablespoons olive oil, the water, lemon juice, garlic, $1/2$ teaspoon salt and $1/8$ teaspoon pepper in a food processor and process for 10 seconds or until smooth. Add the remaining beans and rosemary and pulse just until mixed but not smooth.

Whisk 1 tablespoon olive oil, the vinegar, $1/4$ teaspoon salt and $1/8$ teaspoon pepper in a bowl. Add the onion and arugula and toss to coat. Spread the bean mixture on 1 side of each toasted bread slice and top each with some of the onion mixture. Serve immediately.

Baked Brie with Garlic Fig Compote

Serves 12

1 large round Brie cheese
1 (8-ounce) jar fig spread or fig preserves
1 tablespoon minced garlic

1 tablespoon balsamic vinegar or fig
   balsamic vinegar
12 slices crusty bread

*P*reheat the oven to 350 degrees. Cut the Brie horizontally into 2 equal portions. Combine the fig spread, garlic and vinegar in a bowl and mix well. Spread the fig mixture over the cut side of 1 of the Brie halves and top with the remaining half cut side down. Place the Brie on a baking sheet and surround with the bread slices in a single layer. Bake for 10 minutes or until the Brie is soft and the bread slices are light brown. Serve immediately. If fig spread or fig preserves are not available, process 6 dried California figs with a small amount of boiling water in a food processor until puréed.

Caviar Pie

Serves 8 to 10

4 hard-cooked eggs
1/4 cup (1/2 stick) butter, softened
1 onion, finely chopped
2 cans flat anchovies, drained
1 tablespoon mayonnaise

2 tablespoons chopped fresh Italian parsley
1 (4-ounce) jar caviar
Juice of 1/2 lemon
1 cup sour cream
Chopped fresh Italian parsley to taste

*M*ash the eggs in a bowl. Add the butter and 1/2 of the onion and mix well. Spread the egg mixture over the bottom of a 9-inch round dish. Chill for 30 minutes or longer.

Mash the anchovies in a bowl and stir in the mayonnaise and 2 tablespoons parsley. Spread the anchovy mixture over the egg mixture. Mix the caviar, remaining onion and lemon juice in a bowl and spread over the prepared layers. Top with the sour cream just before serving and sprinkle with parsley to taste. Serve with assorted party crackers or party bread. You may prepare in advance and store in the refrigerator, topping with the sour cream and sprinkling with parsley just before serving.

Potage Crécy

Serves 4

4 carrots, peeled and chopped (about 3 cups)
1/4 cup chopped yellow onion
2 teaspoons minced fresh gingerroot
2 tablespoons unsalted butter
1 russet potato, peeled and chopped

24 to 28 ounces chicken stock or
 vegetable stock
2 teaspoons chopped fresh dill weed
Salt and pepper to taste
Heavy cream (optional)

*S*auté the carrots, onion and gingerroot in the butter in a saucepan over medium heat for 3 to 4 minutes. Stir in the potato and stock; reduce the heat. Simmer until the potato is tender, stirring occasionally. Strain, reserving the solids and liquid.

Combine the reserved solids and dill weed in a blender. Add just enough of the reserved liquid to cover and process until blended, adding additional reserved liquid if needed for the desired consistency. The soup should be pourable, but thicker than heavy cream.

Return the soup to the saucepan and season with salt and pepper. Stir in the desired amount of heavy cream and heat just until warm, stirring frequently; do not boil. Ladle into soup bowls.

Roasted Butternut Squash Soup

Chipotle in adobo sauce can be found in the Mexican section of most supermarkets.

Serves 6

1½ pounds butternut squash
2 tablespoons unsalted butter, softened
¼ teaspoon nutmeg
1 tablespoon unsalted butter
2 pears, peeled and coarsely chopped
¼ cup coarsely chopped celery
¼ cup coarsely chopped onion
1 teaspoon salt
1¾ cups chicken stock
1¾ cups water
2 tablespoons unsalted butter
Salt and pepper to taste
2 tablespoons heavy cream (optional)
½ teaspoon chipotle in adobo sauce, or to taste (optional)

*P*reheat the oven to 450 degrees. Cut the squash horizontally into halves and scoop out the seeds. Rub the pulp with 2 tablespoons butter and sprinkle with the nutmeg. Arrange the squash halves cut side up on a baking sheet and cover with foil. Bake for 1 hour or until tender. Let stand until cool.

Heat 1 tablespoon butter in a medium saucepan over medium-low heat. Add the pears, celery, onion and 1 teaspoon salt to the butter and cook for 5 minutes or until the celery and onion are tender, stirring frequently; do not brown.

Heat the stock and water in a stockpot. Scoop the cooled squash pulp into the stock mixture and simmer for 15 minutes, stirring occasionally. Heat 2 tablespoons butter in a small saucepan over medium heat until nut brown in color and stir into the stock mixture. Add the pear mixture and mix well.

Process the soup in batches in a blender or with a cordless hand mixer until puréed and season with salt and pepper to taste. Ladle into soup bowls. Or, you may strain the soup through a fine sieve into a bowl and stir in the heavy cream and chipotle in adobo sauce. Season with salt and pepper and ladle into soup bowls.

*I*n 1938, a small group of Valley citizens gathered in Papago Park to create a botanical garden whose precepts would encourage an understanding, appreciation, and promotion of the uniqueness of the world's deserts, particularly the Sonoran Desert. They foresaw the Valley's potential and unique identity, envisioning the need to conserve their beautiful desert environment. The Desert Botanical Garden, since its inception in 1939, continues to be a testament to their vision.

Nestled amid the red buttes of Papago Park, the Desert Botanical Garden hosts one of the world's finest collections of desert plants. One of only forty-four botanical gardens accredited by the American Association of Museums, this one-of-a-kind museum showcases fifty acres of beautiful outdoor exhibits. Home to 139 rare, threatened, and endangered plant species from around the world, the Garden offers interesting and inspiring experiences to more than 250,000 visitors each year.

Creamy Shellfish Soup

Serves 2 to 4

2 large shallots, minced
2 garlic cloves, minced
2 tablespoons butter
1/2 cup white wine
1/4 teaspoon celery seeds
1/4 teaspoon Hungarian paprika
Salt and white pepper to taste
1 cup clam juice
2 tablespoons tomato paste
2 teaspoons Worcestershire sauce
1 teaspoon horseradish sauce, or to taste
12 ounces shrimp, peeled, deveined and chopped
1 cup half-and-half or cream
1 teaspoon hot sauce, or to taste
1 teaspoon lemon juice, or to taste
Minced fresh parsley to taste

Decorate liquor bottles for the holidays! Start by placing the bottle in a clean one-half gallon paper milk carton. Surround the bottle with fresh cranberries, pine needles, and water and freeze until firm. When ready to use, remove the paper carton and set the bottle on the bar for your guests to enjoy.

Sweat the shallots and garlic in the butter in a medium saucepan for 2 minutes. Stir in the wine, celery seeds, paprika, salt and white pepper. Cook for 1 minute, stirring occasionally. Add the clam juice, tomato paste, Worcestershire sauce and horseradish sauce and mix well. Bring to a boil; reduce the heat.

Simmer, covered, for 10 to 15 minutes, stirring occasionally. Add the shrimp and cook for 2 minutes or until the shrimp turn pink, stirring occasionally. Reduce the heat to low and stir in the half-and-half, hot sauce and lemon juice. Cook just until heated through; do not boil. Taste and adjust the seasonings. Ladle into soup bowls and sprinkle with parsley. You may substitute lobster meat for the shrimp.

Festive Arugula Salad with Oranges, Pomegranate Seeds and Goat Cheese

Serves 10 to 12

Citrus Dressing
3/4 cup extra-virgin olive oil
1/4 cup fresh lemon juice
2 tablespoons orange juice
2 tablespoons red wine vinegar
1 teaspoon sugar
3/4 teaspoon coarse salt

Salad
5 oranges
14 ounces arugula, trimmed (about 16 cups)
3/4 cup pomegranate seeds or dried cranberries
5 ounces soft fresh goat cheese, crumbled
1/3 cup finely chopped red onion
1/4 cup pine nuts, toasted

*F*or the dressing, combine the olive oil, lemon juice, orange juice, vinegar, sugar and salt in a jar with a tight-fitting lid and seal tightly. Shake to mix.

For the salad, peel the oranges and remove the white pith. Cut the oranges into 1/4- to 1/2-inch rounds and cut each round into quarters. Combine the orange quarters, arugula, pomegranate seeds, cheese and onion in a bowl and mix well. Add the desired amount of dressing and toss to coat. Sprinkle with the pine nuts before serving.

Jicama Pomegranate Salad

Decrease the amount of preparation time by purchasing packaged jicama and pomegranate seeds at specialty markets.

Serves 6

1 large pomegranate
1 pound jicama, peeled and grated
2 tablespoons finely shredded fresh mint
3 tablespoons fresh lime juice

*C*ut the pomegranate into quarters and gently remove the seeds, discarding the yellowish membrane. Combine the pomegranate seeds, jicama, mint and lime juice in a bowl and toss gently. Serve at room temperature or chilled.

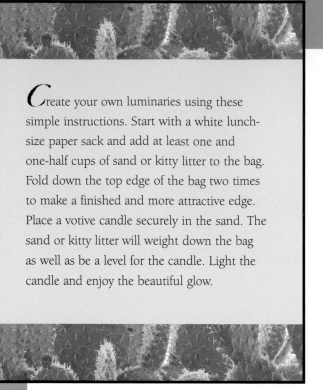

Create your own luminaries using these simple instructions. Start with a white lunch-size paper sack and add at least one and one-half cups of sand or kitty litter to the bag. Fold down the top edge of the bag two times to make a finished and more attractive edge. Place a votive candle securely in the sand. The sand or kitty litter will weight down the bag as well as be a level for the candle. Light the candle and enjoy the beautiful glow.

Baked Apricots

Serves 8 to 10

5 (15-ounce) cans peeled apricot halves
1 (16-ounce) package brown sugar
3/4 to 1 cup (1 1/2 to 2 sticks) butter or margarine
1 sleeve butter crackers, crushed

Preheat the oven to 300 degrees. Drain the apricots, reserving the juice from 1 can. Layer the apricots 2 halves at a time in a 9×13-inch baking pan sprayed with nonstick cooking spray. Layer with the brown sugar and dot with the butter. Pour the reserved juice over the top and sprinkle with the cracker crumbs.

Bake for 45 to 60 minutes or until brown and bubbly. Serve with baked or fried chicken, pork chops or turkey. You may prepare up to 1 day in advance and store, covered, in the refrigerator, increasing the baking time by approximately 10 minutes. Substitute a mixture of pineapple chunks, mandarin oranges and sliced peaches for the apricots for a different twist.

Sautéed Haricots Verts, Red Bell Peppers and Pine Nuts

It would not be Christmas without some red and green on the table.

Serves 8

1 1/2 pounds haricots verts or other slender
   green beans, trimmed
Salt to taste
1 1/2 tablespoons olive oil
2 red bell peppers, cut into 1/2-inch pieces

3 tablespoons butter
2 garlic cloves, minced
1/2 cup pine nuts, toasted
Pepper to taste

Cook the beans in boiling salted water in a saucepan for 4 minutes or until tender-crisp. Drain and immediately plunge the beans into a bowl of ice water to stop the cooking process; drain.

Heat the olive oil in a skillet over medium-high heat. Sauté the bell peppers in the hot oil for 5 minutes or just until tender. Add the butter and heat until melted. Stir in the garlic and sauté for 1 minute or until fragrant. Add the beans and sauté for 5 minutes or until heated through. Stir in the pine nuts and season with salt and pepper. Serve immediately as a side dish or chill and serve as a salad.

Mushroom and Orzo Pilaf

To save time, slice the mushrooms with an egg slicer.

Serves 6 to 8

3 tablespoons butter
2 large shallots, chopped
1 tablespoon chopped fresh thyme
2 large garlic cloves, chopped
12 ounces assorted mushrooms, sliced
3 tablespoons butter

12 ounces orzo (1^2/$_3$ cups)
3^1/$_2$ cups chicken broth
^{1}/$_8$ teaspoon nutmeg
1 teaspoon chopped fresh thyme
Salt and pepper to taste

*M*elt 3 tablespoons butter in a large skillet over medium-high heat. Add the shallots, 1 tablespoon thyme and garlic to the butter and sauté for 1 minute. Stir in the mushrooms and sauté for 8 minutes or until tender but not brown. Add 3 tablespoons butter and the pasta and mix well. Stir in the broth and nutmeg. Bring to a boil; reduce the heat to medium-low. Cook, covered, for 15 minutes or until the pasta is tender and the broth is absorbed. Stir in 1 teaspoon thyme, salt and pepper. Serve immediately.

Twice-Baked Gorgonzola Potatoes

Serves 4

16 small red potatoes
Olive oil to taste
Salt and ground pepper to taste
^{1}/$_3$ cup crumbled Gorgonzola cheese

^{1}/$_4$ cup sour cream
1 tablespoon thinly sliced fresh chives
1 tablespoon butter, softened

*P*reheat the oven to 375 degrees. Cut a small slice off the bottom of each potato to allow the potatoes to stand upright. Coat each potato lightly with olive oil and season lightly with salt and pepper. Arrange the potatoes in a single layer in a baking pan and roast for 30 minutes or until tender, turning occasionally. Cool slightly. Cut off the top quarter of each potato. Scoop out most of the potato pulp, leaving a thin shell. Combine the potato pulp, cheese, sour cream, chives and butter in a mixing bowl and beat until combined.

Preheat the broiler. Spoon some of the potato filling into each potato shell and arrange the potatoes stuffing side up on a baking sheet. Broil until light brown. Serve immediately.

Stuffed Tomatoes

Serves 4

4 vine-ripened red or yellow tomatoes
Extra-virgin olive oil to taste
Salt and freshly ground pepper to taste
2 cups arugula leaves (about 1 bunch)
1/2 cup bread crumbs

1/2 cup (2 ounces) grated
   Parmigiano-Reggiano cheese
1 tablespoon extra-virgin olive oil
1/4 to 1/2 teaspoon red pepper flakes, crushed
1 garlic clove

*C*ut a thin slice from the top of each tomato and discard. Scoop out the pulp and seeds and invert the tomatoes onto a paper towel to drain. Arrange the tomato shells cut side up on a lightly buttered broiler pan. Drizzle with olive oil to taste and sprinkle with salt and pepper. Preheat the oven to 400 degrees. Combine the arugula, bread crumbs, cheese, 1 tablespoon olive oil, red pepper flakes and garlic in a food processor and pulse just until ground and the consistency of a stuffing. Spoon the stuffing into the tomato shells and place the pan on the middle oven rack. Bake for 10 to 12 minutes or until light brown. Let stand for 5 minutes before serving. You may substitute fresh spinach, fresh basil or your favorite greens for the arugula.

Risotto Milanese

Serves 8

6 cups beef, chicken or vegetable broth
6 tablespoons butter
1 small onion, finely chopped
2 cups arborio rice

1/2 cup white wine
1/2 teaspoon saffron threads
1/2 cup (2 ounces) grated Parmesan cheese
Salt and pepper to taste

*B*ring the broth to a boil in a saucepan. Remove from the heat and cover to keep warm. Heat the butter in a saucepan over medium heat. Add the onion to the butter and cook for 5 minutes or until tender, stirring constantly with a wooden spoon. Stir in the rice and cook for 3 minutes, stirring constantly until every grain is coated. Add the wine and mix well.

Cook for 5 minutes or until reduced, stirring frequently. Add 1 cup of the warm broth to the rice mixture and cook until the liquid is absorbed, stirring constantly. Add the remaining warm broth 1 cup at a time, cooking until the liquid has been absorbed after each addition and stirring constantly. Stir in the saffron after 10 minutes. The process will take about 20 minutes for the rice to absorb all of the broth and to become tender. Remove from the heat and stir in the cheese and season with salt and pepper. Serve with Osso Buco on page 208.

Herbed Beef Tenderloin with Red Wine Sauce

Serves 6 to 8

Beef Tenderloin

1 (6-pound) beef tenderloin, trimmed of
    chain and fat
1/4 cup olive oil
1/4 cup chopped fresh rosemary
1/4 cup chopped fresh Italian parsley
1/4 cup chopped fresh thyme
6 garlic cloves, minced
1 tablespoon kosher salt
1 tablespoon freshly ground pepper

Red Wine Sauce

2 tablespoons unsalted butter
6 shallots, thinly sliced
1 garlic clove, minced
2 cups full-bodied dry red wine
2 tablespoons red wine vinegar
4 cups beef broth
5 sprigs of thyme
1/4 cup tomato concassée
3 tablespoons unsalted butter
1 tablespoon chopped fresh Italian parsley
Salt and pepper to taste

*F*or the tenderloin, coat the tenderloin with the olive oil. Mix the rosemary, parsley, thyme and garlic in a bowl and pat over the surface. Sprinkle with the salt and pepper.

Wrap the tenderloin in plastic wrap and chill for 2 to 10 hours.

Preheat the oven to 400 degrees. Sear the tenderloin in an ovenproof skillet or Dutch oven for 15 minutes or until brown on all sides, turning occasionally. Roast for 30 minutes or until a meat thermometer inserted into the thickest portion of the tenderloin registers 145 degrees for medium-rare. Let rest for 30 minutes before slicing.

For the sauce, melt 2 tablespoons butter in a sauté pan over medium heat. Add the shallots and garlic to the butter and cook for 10 minutes or until the shallots are tender, stirring frequently. Increase the heat to high and stir in the wine and vinegar. Cook for 10 minutes to reduce, stirring frequently. Stir in the broth and thyme and cook for 20 minutes or until the mixture is reduced to 1 cup, stirring frequently. Strain into a bowl, discarding the solids. Let stand until cool.

To serve, reheat the sauce until hot. Whisk in the tomato concassée, 3 tablespoons butter and parsley. Season with salt and pepper. Slice the beef as desired and serve with the sauce. Concassée is a mixture of peeled, seeded and chopped tomatoes.

Osso Buco with Gremolata

Serves 6

Osso Buco
6 veal shanks with bone, 2 inches thick
1/2 cup flour
Salt and pepper to taste
3 tablespoons olive oil
3 tablespoons butter
1 onion, chopped
1/2 cup chopped celery
1/2 cup chopped carrots
4 garlic cloves, coarsely chopped
3 tablespoons finely chopped fresh
   Italian parsley

2 bay leaves
1 cup dry white wine
2 cups veal stock or beef broth
1 cup tomato sauce
Olive oil to taste

Gremolata
Grated zest of 1 lemon
Grated zest of 1 orange
2 garlic cloves, minced
2 tablespoons chopped fresh Italian parsley

*F*or the osso buco, tie a 12-inch piece of kitchen twine around the center of each shank to help retain the shape while braising. Snip off the excess twine at the knot. Adjust the shape of the shank by gently rolling or patting it with your hand until the appearance and thickness are more uniform.

Mix the flour, salt and pepper in a shallow dish. Coat the veal with the flour mixture, tapping off the excess. Heat 3 tablespoons olive oil and the butter in a heavy skillet or Dutch oven over medium heat. Sear the veal in the hot oil mixture until brown on all sides, adding additional olive oil and butter as needed. Remove the veal to a platter, reserving the pan drippings.

Add the onion, celery, carrots, garlic, parsley and bay leaves to the reserved pan drippings and cook until the vegetables are tender, stirring frequently. Season with salt and pepper. Increase the heat to high and deglaze the pan with the wine. Return the veal to the skillet and stir in the stock and tomato sauce and drizzle with olive oil to taste. Reduce the heat to low.

Simmer, covered, for 3 hours or until the veal is tender, basting the veal with the pan juices occasionally. Remove the cover and simmer for 10 minutes longer to slightly reduce the sauce, stirring occasionally. Discard the bay leaves.

For the gremolata, toss the lemon zest, orange zest, garlic and parsley in a bowl and sprinkle over the osso buco. Serve with risotto or polenta.

Pork Tenderloin with Balsamic Cranberry Sauce

Serves 6

Pork Tenderloins

2 (8- to 10-ounce) pork tenderloins
Salt and pepper to taste

Balsamic Cranberry Sauce and Assembly

1 tablespoon olive oil
1 onion, chopped
1 shallot, minced
2 garlic cloves, minced
1 tablespoon chopped fresh rosemary
1 (16-ounce) can whole cranberry sauce
1 cup canned reduced-sodium chicken broth
1/4 cup balsamic vinegar
1 tablespoon butter
Salt and pepper to taste
1 tablespoon chopped fresh parsley

*F*or the tenderloins, preheat the grill. Sprinkle the tenderloins with salt and pepper. Arrange the tenderloins on the grill rack and grill over hot coals for 20 minutes or until a meat thermometer inserted in the center registers 160 degrees. Remove from the grill and let rest for 10 minutes.

For the sauce, heat the olive oil in a skillet over medium heat. Sauté the onion, shallot, garlic and rosemary in the hot oil for 3 to 5 minutes or until the onion is tender. Mix in the cranberry sauce, broth and vinegar.

Cook for 2 minutes or until the cranberry sauce melts, whisking constantly. Bring to a boil and boil for 6 minutes or until thickened, stirring frequently. Stir in the butter, salt and pepper. To serve, slice the pork and serve with the sauce. Sprinkle with the parsley.

Sausage Spinach Wreath with Apple Salsa

Serves 10 to 12

Apple Salsa

3 tablespoons sugar
1^{1}/$_{2}$ tablespoons cider vinegar
1^{1}/$_{2}$ tablespoons lemon juice
^{1}/$_{8}$ to ^{1}/$_{4}$ teaspoon red pepper flakes
3 sweet apples (Golden Delicious), peeled and chopped
1 teaspoon minced fresh oregano, or ^{1}/$_{2}$ teaspoon
    dried oregano

Sausage Spinach Wreath

1 (10-ounce) package frozen chopped spinach, thawed
    and drained
12 ounces seasoned bulk pork sausage
1 loaf frozen bread dough, thawed
1 cup (4 ounces) shredded Cheddar cheese
Garlic powder to taste

*F*or the salsa, bring the sugar, vinegar, lemon juice and red pepper flakes to a boil in a saucepan over high heat, stirring occasionally. Stir in the apples and reduce the heat to low. Simmer, covered, until the apples are tender, stirring occasionally. Remove from the heat and mash the apple mixture until almost smooth. Stir in the oregano. Spoon the salsa into a bowl and chill, covered, in the refrigerator.

For the wreath, preheat the oven to 350 degrees. Press the excess moisture from the spinach. Brown the sausage in a skillet, stirring until crumbly; drain. Roll the dough into an 8×13-inch rectangle on a lightly floured surface. Layer with the sausage, spinach and cheese and sprinkle with garlic powder. Beginning with 1 of the long sides, roll to enclose the filling.

Arrange the roll seam side down on a greased baking sheet and shape into a wreath, pinching the ends together. Bake for 20 to 25 minutes or until golden brown. Slice and serve with the salsa and/or flavored mustards. Garnish with fresh holly if creating a holiday look.

Cornish Game Hens with Apple Plum Stuffing

Serves 4

Cornish Game Hens

2 (1½- to 1¾-pound) frozen Cornish game
   hens, thawed and cut into halves
2 teaspoons thyme
Salt and pepper to taste
¼ cup olive oil

Apple Plum Stuffing

2 tablespoons unsalted butter
½ cup chopped yellow onion
2 garlic cloves, minced
1 cup chopped celery

1 Red Delicious apple, chopped
2 links sweet or spicy sausage, casings removed
1 tablespoon sage
1 tablespoon rosemary
Salt and pepper to taste
1 cup whole wheat bread cubes
1 cup dark rye bread cubes
1 cup white bread cubes
1 cup chopped plums or plum preserves
3 cups chicken broth
2 cups (8 ounces) grated Parmesan cheese
Melted unsalted butter (optional)

*F*or the game hens, preheat the oven to 500 degrees. Sprinkle the game hens with the thyme, salt and pepper. Heat the olive oil in a large skillet over medium-high heat. Arrange the game hen halves skin side down in the hot oil. Cook for 6 minutes per side or until brown, turning once. Remove the game hen halves to a baking pan, reserving the pan drippings. Roast for 20 minutes or until the juices run clear when the thigh is lightly pierced with a fork.

For the stuffing, preheat the oven to 350 degrees. Heat the reserved pan drippings with 2 tablespoons butter until hot. Sauté the onion and garlic in the butter mixture for 3 to 4 minutes. Stir in the celery, apple, sausage, sage and rosemary. Cook for 30 minutes to allow the flavors to marry and season with salt and pepper.

Spoon the apple mixture into a bowl and add the bread cubes, plums and enough broth for a moist but not sticky stuffing. Stir in the cheese. Spoon the stuffing into a baking pan and drizzle with melted butter. Bake for 40 to 45 minutes or until brown and bubbly. Serve with the game hens. You may substitute any variety of breads for the ones mentioned.

Decorating with pomegranates is a fresh idea to spice up your holiday table and wreaths. Experiment with a pomegranate on a holiday wreath. Just thread floral wire through the crown of the fruit and tie to your wreath. For larger pomegranates, you may need to use two wires. Drying pomegranates is a simple task; you just need to plan ahead. Place the fruit on a wire rack; do not allow them to touch. Find an area with proper air circulation and allow the fruit to dry for several weeks. Once the fruit are dry, set them on a table and add evergreen branches, pinecones, and poinsettia flowers to create an artful display. To bring out the vibrant red color of pomegranates, rub the surface with a small amount of vegetable oil. The shine draws your eye immediately to the table setting or wreath in which you have included the fruit.

Baked Apples with Marsala-Soaked Raisins

Serves 4

4 apples, cored and peeled
$1/4$ cup ($1/2$ stick) unsalted butter, melted
3 tablespoons sugar
3 tablespoons cinnamon
$1/4$ cup ($1/2$ stick) unsalted butter, cut into tablespoons
1 cup golden raisins
1 cup marsala

Preheat the oven to 400 degrees. Coat the apples with the melted butter and roll in a mixture of the sugar and cinnamon. Arrange the apples in a lightly greased baking pan and place 1 tablespoon of the $1/4$ cup butter in each apple center. Bake, covered with foil, for 1 hour or until very tender. Combine the raisins and wine in a saucepan and simmer until the raisins are plump and the wine is reduced, stirring occasionally.

To serve, arrange 1 apple on each of 4 dessert plates. Drain the raisins and spoon evenly into the apple centers. Serve with a scoop of vanilla ice cream. You may combine the leftover wine, a few tablespoons of sugar and 1 teaspoon cinnamon in a saucepan and cook until reduced and thickened. Drizzle over the apples.

Eggnog Ice Cream

Makes 4 1/2 cups

1/2 cup bourbon (optional)
2 cups milk
1 1/4 cups sugar

8 egg yolks, beaten
2 cups heavy cream
3/4 teaspoon nutmeg

*B*ring the bourbon to a simmer in a 10-inch skillet over high heat. Remove from the heat and ignite. Shake gently until the flame subsides. Combine the milk and sugar in a saucepan and bring to a simmer over high heat. Remove from the heat and whisk a small amount of the hot mixture into the egg yolks. Whisk the egg yolks into the hot mixture.

Cook over low heat for 6 to 9 minutes or until the custard coats the back of a spoon, stirring constantly. Remove from the heat and stir in the bourbon, heavy cream and nutmeg. Strain the custard through a fine sieve into a large metal bowl, discarding the residue. Place the metal bowl in a larger bowl filled with ice. Let stand for 15 minutes or until cold, stirring frequently.

Pour the custard into an ice cream freezer container and freeze using the manufacturer's directions. Scoop the ice cream into bowls, or for a firmer ice cream, store in an airtight container in the freezer for at least 3 hours or for up to 1 week.

Almond Roca

Makes 2 pounds

8 ounces sliced almonds
8 ounces milk chocolate, chilled and broken
  into chunks

2 cups (4 sticks) butter
2 cups sugar

*P*ulse the almonds in a food processor until chopped. Remove the almonds to a bowl. Place the chocolate in a food processor and pulse until finely chopped. Spread 1/2 of the almonds in a 10×15-inch baking pan and sprinkle with 1/2 of the chocolate. Combine the butter and sugar in a large microwave-safe bowl. Using a large bowl is critical as the mixture will double in volume. Microwave on High for 2 minutes and whisk until blended. Microwave on High for 4 minutes and whisk until smooth.

Continue to Microwave on High for 8 to 12 minutes longer or until the mixture is a rich golden brown, stirring only as necessary to even out the color. Pour over the prepared layers, sprinkle with the remaining chocolate and almonds and gently press. Score the candy while warm. Let stand until cool and break into irregular pieces. Store in an airtight container.

Bourbon Pumpkin Cheesecake

Serves 12 to 14

Pecan Crust

3/4 cup graham cracker crumbs

1/2 cup pecans, finely chopped

1/4 cup packed light brown sugar

1/4 cup sugar

1/4 cup (1/2 stick) unsalted butter, melted
  and cooled

Pumpkin Filling

1 1/2 cups canned solid-pack pumpkin

3 eggs

1/2 cup packed light brown sugar

2 tablespoons heavy cream

1 tablespoon bourbon liqueur or bourbon
  (optional)

1 teaspoon vanilla extract

1/2 cup sugar

1 tablespoon cornstarch

1 1/2 teaspoons cinnamon

1/2 teaspoon freshly grated nutmeg

1/2 teaspoon ginger

1/2 teaspoon salt

24 ounces cream cheese, softened

Topping

2 cups sour cream

2 tablespoons sugar

1 tablespoon bourbon liqueur or bourbon
  (optional)

*F*or the crust, invert the bottom of a 9-inch springform pan to create a flat bottom and lock the side. Coat the bottom and side with butter. Combine the graham cracker crumbs, pecans, brown sugar, sugar and 1/4 cup butter in a bowl and mix well. Press the crumb mixture over the bottom and 1/2 inch up the side of the prepared pan. Chill for 1 hour.

For the filling, position the oven rack in the center of the oven and preheat the oven to 350 degrees. Whisk the pumpkin, eggs, brown sugar, heavy cream, liqueur and vanilla in a bowl until blended. Mix the sugar, cornstarch, cinnamon, nutmeg, ginger and salt in a mixing bowl. Add the cream cheese to the cornstarch mixture and beat at high speed for 3 minutes or until creamy and smooth. Add the pumpkin mixture to the cream cheese mixture and beat at medium speed until smooth.

Spoon the filling over the chilled crust and arrange the springform pan in a shallow baking pan. Bake for 50 to 60 minutes or just until the center is set. Cool on a wire rack for 5 minutes. Maintain the oven temperature.

For the topping, whisk the sour cream, sugar and liqueur in a bowl until blended and spread over the top of the cheesecake. Bake for 5 minutes. Remove to a wire rack and let stand for 3 hours or until cool. Chill, covered, for 4 hours or until cold.

To serve, remove the side of the pan and bring the cheesecake to room temperature before slicing. You may prepare up to 2 days in advance and store, covered, in the refrigerator.

Bacardi Rum Cake

Serves 16

Rum Cake

1 cup chopped pecans or walnuts
1 (2-layer) package yellow cake mix
1 (4-ounce) package lemon instant
   pudding mix
4 eggs
1/2 cup cold water
1/2 cup vegetable oil
1/2 cup dark Bacardi rum

Rum Glaze and Assembly

1/2 cup (1 stick) butter
1 cup sugar
1/4 cup water
1/2 cup dark Bacardi rum
Confectioners' sugar to taste

*F*or the cake, preheat the oven to 325 degrees. Grease and flour a bundt pan. Sprinkle the pecans over the bottom of the prepared pan. Combine the cake mix, pudding mix, eggs, water, oil and rum in a mixing bowl and beat until blended, scraping the bowl occasionally. Spoon the batter over the pecans. Bake for 1 hour. Remove to a wire rack to cool.

For the glaze, heat the butter in a saucepan until melted. Stir in the sugar and water. Bring to a boil and boil for 5 minutes, stirring occasionally. Stir in the rum.

To serve, invert the cooled cake onto a cake platter. Pierce the top with a wooden pick and drizzle with the warm glaze. Let stand until cool and dust lightly with confectioners' sugar.

Celebrated Chefs

Front left to right: Barbara Pool Fenzl, Les Gourmettes Cooking School; Silvana Salcido Esparza, Barrio Café; Charles Wiley, elements; Gabriel Baza, Mancuso's.

Back left to right: Matthew Carter, Zinc Bistro; Robert McGrath, Roaring Fork; John Conrad II, The Arizona Kitchen at the Wigwam Resort & Golf Club; Fernando Divina, LON's at the hermosa; Robert Graham, Bistro 24 at The Ritz-Carlton; Bernie Kantak, Cowboy Ciao; Kenneth Giordano, Durant's; Franco Fazzuoli, Franco's Italian Caffé; Jeff Blake, Arcadia Farms.

Not pictured: James Robert, Eddie V's Edgewater Grill

The Valley of the Sun is one of the fastest growing cities in the country, attracting award-winning chefs with diverse culinary backgrounds. Phoenix lays claim to many James Beard Award nominees each year, a testament to the outstanding group of culinary professionals throughout our city. There is a wonderful array of food, ranging from causal to traditional, Southwestern to French, and everything in between. Menus are fresh with a modern, sophisticated flair. These professionals have put Phoenix on the culinary map. The generosity of these contributing chefs provides inspiration to discover the chef within us all.

Celebrated Chefs

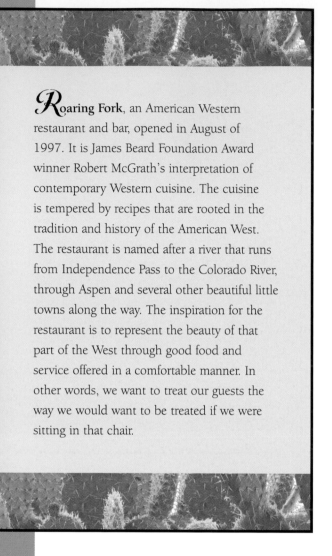

Alaskan King Crab and Avocado Salad with Roasted Garlic Mayonnaise

Chef Robert McGrath of Roaring Fork contributed this recipe.

Serves 4

Roasted Garlic Mayonnaise
2 tablespoons garlic cloves
1 tablespoon extra-virgin olive oil
3/4 cup mayonnaise
2 tablespoons lemon juice

Salad
1 pound chopped steamed king crab meat
2 cups chopped avocados
1 cup fresh cilantro leaves
1/2 cup chopped ripe tomato
Kosher salt and cracked pepper to taste
2 cups arugula leaves

For the mayonnaise, preheat the oven to 325 degrees. Toss the garlic with the olive oil in a small baking pan and roast for 10 minutes or until golden brown, stirring occasionally. Mash the garlic in a bowl with a fork until smooth. Add the mayonnaise and lemon juice to the garlic and mix well.

For the salad, combine the crab meat, avocados, cilantro and tomato in a bowl and mix gently. Add the mayonnaise and toss to coat. Season with salt and pepper. Spoon the crab meat mixture over the arugula on 4 serving plates.

 Sportsman's Fine Wines and Spirits recommends: This works well with a good Italian Arneis, my favorite being Ceretto "Blange," Langhe, Italy.

Tiramisù

Legend has it that the tiramisù, translated as "pick me up" in Italian, was the favorite of Venice's courtesans, who needed a "pick me up" to fortify themselves between amorous encounters. This may not be true, but it makes for a colorful history. Chef Franco Fazzuoli of Franco's Italian Caffé contributed this recipe.

Serves 12

1/2 cup sugar
2 1/2 cups espresso
3/4 cup brandy
3/4 cup amaretto
100 (about) ladyfingers (preferably Italian)
8 egg yolks, lightly beaten
1/2 cup sugar
1 1/2 (17-ounce) containers mascarpone cheese
  (preferably imported)
8 egg whites
2 tablespoons sugar
2/3 cup (4 ounces) semisweet chocolate chips, finely chopped
2 cups whipping cream, whipped

Franco Fazzuoli, owner and general manager of **Franco's Italian Caffé** in Phoenix, Arizona, was born in Florence, Italy. At the age of twenty-five, Franco moved to New York City, where he lived for twenty years and opened three critically acclaimed Italian restaurants, Cent' Anni, Il Ponte Vecchio, and Zinno. In 1987, Franco moved to Phoenix, where he has owned and operated Franco's Trattoria and the new Franco's Italian Caffé. Franco, along with Executive Chef Steve Martin, specializes in hearty and flavorful Tuscan cuisine, such as chicken paillard, rotisserie meats, homemade pastas, and wood-oven pizzas. Franco's celebrates the cuisine of northern Italy in a casual, comfortable atmosphere at competitive prices.

Dissolve 1/2 cup sugar in the espresso in a bowl. Stir in the brandy and amaretto. Dip the ladyfingers in the espresso mixture for about 3 seconds. Cook the egg yolks in a double boiler until a thermometer registers 165 degrees. Remove from the heat and stir in 1/2 cup sugar and the cheese. Beat the egg whites in a mixing bowl until almost stiff peaks form. Beat in 2 tablespoons sugar.

Cover the bottom of a 9×13-inch dish with 1/2 of the ladyfingers. Layer with 1/2 of the meringue, 1/2 of the cheese mixture and 1/2 of the chocolate chips. Top with the remaining ladyfingers, remaining meringue and remaining cheese mixture. Spread with the whipped cream and sprinkle with the remaining chocolate chips. Chill, covered, in the refrigerator until serving time. The traditional Florentine tiramisù is meant to be very moist and liquidy, not dry.

 Sportsman's Fine Wines and Spirits recommends: The wine has to be the traditional Italian dessert wine "Vin Santo." One of the best is Lungarotti "Vin Santo" of Torgiano, Italy.

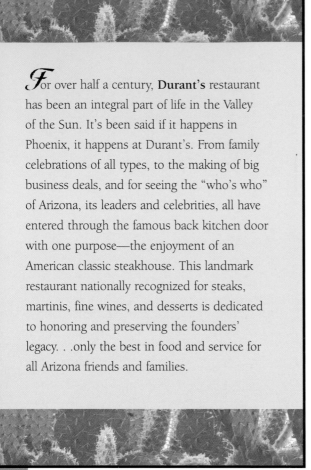

For over half a century, **Durant's** restaurant has been an integral part of life in the Valley of the Sun. It's been said if it happens in Phoenix, it happens at Durant's. From family celebrations of all types, to the making of big business deals, and for seeing the "who's who" of Arizona, its leaders and celebrities, all have entered through the famous back kitchen door with one purpose—the enjoyment of an American classic steakhouse. This landmark restaurant nationally recognized for steaks, martinis, fine wines, and desserts is dedicated to honoring and preserving the founders' legacy. . .only the best in food and service for all Arizona friends and families.

Spinach and Artichoke Dip

Chef Kenneth Giordano of Durant's contributed this recipe.

Makes 8 cups

1 (16-ounce) package frozen chopped spinach, thawed and drained
1 (16-ounce) can artichoke hearts, drained
1 yellow onion, finely chopped
1/2 cup (1 stick) butter
1/2 cup flour
4 cups milk
2 cups heavy cream
1 tablespoon granulated onion
1 tablespoon granulated garlic
1 1/2 teaspoons salt
1/2 teaspoon pepper
1 pound Parmesan cheese, grated

Press the excess moisture from the spinach and artichokes and coarsely chop the artichokes. Sauté the yellow onion in the butter in a sauté pan until tender. Add the flour and cook for 5 minutes, stirring constantly.

Bring the milk, heavy cream, granulated onion, granulated garlic, salt and pepper to a boil in a large saucepan, stirring occasionally. Add the onion mixture gradually, whisking constantly, and bring to a simmer. Stir in the spinach, artichokes and cheese. Simmer until heated through, stirring frequently.

Serve warm with fresh tortilla chips, bread cubes or fresh vegetables. Store leftovers in the refrigerator or freeze for future use. Also great as Oysters Rockefeller, just adding chopped crisp-cooked bacon on top of the oysters and baking until golden brown.

 Sportsman's Fine Wines and Spirits recommends: Another perfect choice for beer. Try Pilsner Urquell from the Czech Republic.

Pistachio Salmon with Amaretto Butter Sauce and Roasted Radicchio

Chef Bernie Kantak of Cowboy Ciao contributed this recipe.

Serves 4

Salmon

2 ounces pistachios

2 tablespoons flour

4 (8-ounce) salmon fillets

Salt and pepper to taste

Olive oil or butter

Roasted Radicchio

1 head radicchio, cut into
    quarters

2 tablespoons olive oil

1 tablespoon sugar

Salt and pepper to taste

Amaretto Butter Sauce

1/4 cup white wine

2 tablespoons amaretto

1 shallot, minced

2 tablespoons heavy cream

1/2 cup (1 stick) butter,
    chilled and cubed

Cowboy Ciao is the heart of downtown Scottsdale's "Restaurant Row." Since 1997, this modern American eatery has featured whimsical décor, caring service, and extensive beverages to enhance the Southwest/Italian-influenced dishes. The maverick wine list (originally 111 varieties, now 2,000 varieties) was honored with the *Wine Spectator* Award of Excellence (or "Best of") every year of operation. The dining renaissance at Stetson and 6th Avenue continues with sister venues Kazimierz world wine bar and Sea Saw, highlighting Chef Nobuo Fukuda's better-than-sushi magic. The Cowboy Ciao "family" has evolved, but the original mission remains true: thrill each guest, every visit, with an entertaining, memorable experience.

For the salmon, preheat the oven to 350 degrees. Process the pistachios and flour in a food processor until ground. Sprinkle the salmon with salt and pepper and coat the bone side with the pistachio mixture, pressing lightly. Sear the salmon in a small amount of olive oil in an ovenproof skillet until light brown. Bake until the salmon flakes easily. Cover to keep warm. Increase the oven temperature to 450 degrees.

For the radicchio, toss the radicchio, olive oil, sugar, salt and pepper in a bowl and spoon into a roasting pan. Roast for 10 minutes or until slightly caramelized, stirring occasionally.

For the sauce, combine the wine, liqueur and shallot in a saucepan and bring to a boil. Boil until the mixture is reduced by 3/4, stirring frequently. Stir in the heavy cream and cook until the mixture is reduced by 1/2, stirring frequently. Whisk in the butter until emulsified. Spoon the sauce over the salmon and radicchio on serving plates.

 Sportsman's Fine Wines and Spirits recommends: How about a Pinot Blanc? Not quite as rich and fruity as Chardonnay and not as crisp and dry as a Sauvignon Blanc. Perfect for those in-between recipes. My pick: Chalone Pinot Blanc, Chalone AVA (California).

*T*hirty-five years ago on April 15, on 7th Avenue north of Missouri, Fran's Italian Fruit Ices opened its doors to give Phoenix a new concept in desserts. Four barstools and a cute, quaint little place brought us to where we are today. Family owned and operated by the Mancuso family, we have four restaurants striving to give Arizona wonderful northern Italian cuisine. While our two **Mancuso's** locations bring fine dining, our two Frankie's locations bring a casual atmosphere with great pizzas, pastas, and sandwiches. We are so ever grateful to all our patrons for the continued support because they brought us to where we are today.

Pesto Sauce

Chef Gabriel Baza of Mancuso's contributed this recipe.

Serves 4

2 cups fresh basil
$^1/_2$ cup (2 ounces) grated Parmesan cheese
$^1/_2$ cup olive oil
2 garlic cloves
3 tablespoons butter
2 tablespoons pine nuts
2 tablespoons grated pecorino Romano cheese
1 teaspoon salt

*C*ombine the basil, Parmesan cheese, olive oil, garlic, butter, pine nuts, Romano cheese and salt in a food processor and process to the desired consistency. Toss the pesto with hot cooked pasta and additional grated Parmesan cheese in a serving bowl. Add chopped cooked chicken or steamed shrimp for a heartier dish.

 Sportsman's Fine Wines and Spirits recommends: A wonderful little white wine called Due Uve by Bertani from the region around Verona. The wine is a blend of Pinot Grigio and Sauvignon Blanc that will go with either chicken or shrimp.

Sautéed Halibut in Wild Mushroom Crust with White Truffle Brown Butter

Chef James Robert of Eddie V's Edgewater Grill contributed this recipe.

Serves 2

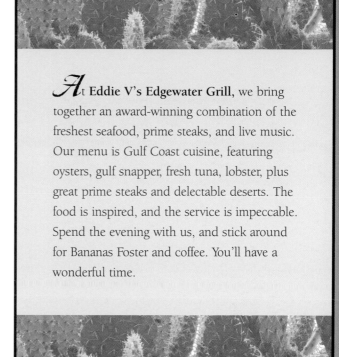

At **Eddie V's Edgewater Grill,** we bring together an award-winning combination of the freshest seafood, prime steaks, and live music. Our menu is Gulf Coast cuisine, featuring oysters, gulf snapper, fresh tuna, lobster, plus great prime steaks and delectable deserts. The food is inspired, and the service is impeccable. Spend the evening with us, and stick around for Bananas Foster and coffee. You'll have a wonderful time.

Wild Mushroom Crust

1/4 cup olive oil
2 shallots, minced
4 garlic cloves, minced
1 cup sliced shiitake
   mushrooms
1 cup sliced oyster
   mushrooms
1 cup sliced button
   mushrooms
1/3 cup brandy
2/3 cup heavy cream
1/3 cup grated
   Parmesan cheese

Halibut

1/2 cup olive oil
2 (6-ounce) halibut fillets
Salt and white pepper
   to taste
Flour

White Truffle Brown Butter and Assembly

2 cups (4 sticks) salted
   butter, cubed
2 tablespoons white
   truffle oil
Fresh chives

For the crust, heat the olive oil in a sauté pan. Add the shallots and garlic to the hot oil and cook until tender and aromatic. Stir in the mushrooms and cook for 10 minutes over medium heat until tender. Add the brandy and cook for 2 minutes or until reduced. Stir in the heavy cream and cook for 3 minutes or until reduced by 1/2. Remove from the heat and stir in the cheese. Cover to keep warm.

For the halibut, preheat the oven to 450 degrees. Heat the olive oil in an ovenproof skillet. Sprinkle the halibut with salt and white pepper and coat with flour. Sauté the halibut in the hot oil until golden brown on both sides, turning once. Spoon 1/2 of the crust over each fillet and bake for 4 minutes.

For the butter, heat a skillet over medium-high heat. Add the butter to the hot skillet and swirl until the butter foams and exudes a nutty aroma. Remove from the heat. To serve, remove the halibut to a serving bowl. Spoon the butter over and around the halibut and drizzle with the truffle oil. Garnish with chives.

 Sportsman's Fine Wines and Spirits recommends: For this awesome rendition of halibut, I would match it with a Sancerre, which is Sauvignon Blanc from the Loire Valley in France. Try Vacheron Sancerre as it's a great match.

Ahi Tuna Niçoise

Chef Matthew Carter of Zinc Bistro contributed this recipe.

Serves 3 to 4

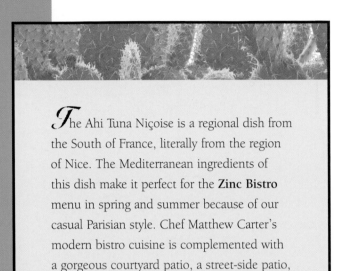

The Ahi Tuna Niçoise is a regional dish from the South of France, literally from the region of Nice. The Mediterranean ingredients of this dish make it perfect for the **Zinc Bistro** menu in spring and summer because of our casual Parisian style. Chef Matthew Carter's modern bistro cuisine is complemented with a gorgeous courtyard patio, a street-side patio, and a twenty-five-foot zinc bar. The oyster and shellfish bar completes the restaurant for a truly authentic Parisian experience.

Ahi Tuna

4 to 6 ounces niçoise olives, pitted

4 garlic cloves

2 or 3 anchovies, soaked in milk and drained

3 or 4 sprigs of fresh parsley

24 to 32 ounces ahi tuna, cut into 3 or 4 (8-ounce) rectangles

Tomato Sauce

2 or 3 garlic cloves, crushed

2 cups chopped ripe organic tomatoes

1 bunch thyme, trimmed and chopped

1 cup chicken stock

1/4 cup extra-virgin olive oil

2 to 3 ounces smoke oil

Salt and pepper to taste

Parsley Sauce

4 to 6 tablespoons extra-virgin olive oil

1/2 to 1 bunch Italian parsley

1 or 2 garlic cloves

Salt and pepper to taste

Fennel Garnish and Assembly

1 or 2 heads fennel, trimmed and thinly shaved

Juice of 4 lemons

1/2 to 1 cup water

1/2 cup sugar

1 to 2 ounces coriander, toasted and crushed

4 to 6 radishes, shaved

1/2 to 1 bunch Italian parsley, trimmed and chopped

Chopped tomatoes to taste

Extra-virgin olive oil to taste

Salt and pepper to taste

For the tuna, preheat the oven to 350 degrees. Process the olives, garlic, anchovies and parsley in a blender until puréed. Rub the tuna on both sides with the tapenade and sear in a hot ovenproof skillet until light brown. Bake until the desired degree of doneness.

For the tomato sauce, brown the garlic in a medium saucepan and stir in the tomatoes and thyme. Cook until the tomatoes are reduced by 1/2 and add the stock. Cook until the mixture is reduced by 1/2, stirring frequently. Process the tomato mixture, olive oil and smoke oil in a blender until incorporated. Press the sauce through a chinois and season with salt and pepper.

For the parsley sauce, process the olive oil, parsley and garlic in a blender until puréed. Season with salt and pepper.

For the garnish, place the fennel in a metal bowl. Bring the lemon juice, water, sugar and coriander to a boil in a saucepan and pour the hot mixture over the fennel. Let stand for 15 minutes to cool.

To serve, spoon a ring of the parsley sauce in the center of 3 or 4 serving plates and fill the rings with the tomato sauce. Slice the tuna widthwise into halves and stack 2 halves showing the temperature towards 6 o'clock on each prepared plate. Toss the drained fennel, radishes, parsley and tomatoes in a bowl. Drizzle with olive oil and season with salt and pepper. Spoon the fennel mixture over the tuna and serve immediately.

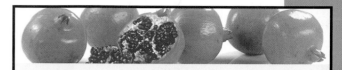

*I*f **Smoke Oil** is not available, set up a small smoker inside a grill or on the stovetop. Soak 6 to 8 ounces wood chips in water for 8 to 10 hours. Preheat the grill on high. Drain the wood chips and arrange on a piece of foil pierced with small holes. Place on the hot coals. Arrange the chopped tomatoes in a flat pan and place on the upper resting rack of the grill. Smoke, with the lid down, for 15 to 20 minutes after the smoke gets thick.

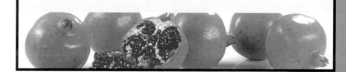

 Sportsman's Fine Wines and Spirits recommends: Rombauer Chardonnay! Fat, rich, and heavy would be a good contrast for this dish. Don't drink it too cold, or all the flavor is lost.

Chicken Tortilla Soup

Chef John Conrad II of The Arizona Kitchen at the Wigwam Resort & Golf Club contributed this recipe.

Serves 8

1/2 cup paprika
1/4 cup cumin, ground
3 tablespoons chili powder
2 tablespoons kosher salt
2 tablespoons coriander, ground
3 pounds chicken breasts, skinned, boned and coarsely chopped
3 tablespoons corn oil
2 white onions, chopped
2 large carrots, chopped
4 ribs celery, chopped
2 ripe tomatoes, coarsely chopped

3 Anaheim chiles, roasted and peeled
2 red bell peppers, roasted and peeled
1/2 gallon chicken stock
12 corn tortillas, cut into quarters
Corn kernels from 4 ears of yellow corn
Salt and pepper to taste
Tortilla chips
Shredded panella cheese
Chopped avocados

Combine the paprika, cumin, chili powder, 2 tablespoons salt and coriander in a shallow dish and mix well. Add the chicken and toss to coat. Cook the chicken in the corn oil in a stockpot until cooked through, stirring frequently. Remove the chicken to a platter using a slotted spoon and reserving the pan drippings. Cook the onions in the reserved pan drippings until tender. Add the carrots and cook for 4 minutes, stirring frequently. Add the celery, tomatoes, Anaheim chiles and bell peppers and mix well. Cook until the celery and bell peppers are tender, stirring frequently. Stir in the stock and bring to a boil; reduce the heat.

Simmer for 20 minutes, stirring occasionally. Remove from the heat and blend the soup with a stick blender or immersion blender until smooth, adding the corn tortillas while blending. Return the stockpot to the heat and stir in the corn. Cook until heated through, stirring occasionally; the soup will begin to thicken. Return the chicken to the stockpot and season with salt and pepper to taste. Cook just until heated through, stirring occasionally. Ladle into soup bowls and top with tortilla chips, panella cheese and avocados.

 Sportsman's Fine Wines and Spirits recommends: While not a good match for wine, a great Mexican beer would be the ticket. My favorite choice would be Negro Modelo.

Blue Corn Bread

*Chef Fernando Divina of LON's at the hermosa contributed
this recipe.*

Serves 15

2 cups whole wheat flour
1 cup yellow cornmeal
1 cup blue cornmeal
1/2 cup sugar
2 tablespoons baking powder
2 teaspoons salt
2 cups milk
1/4 cup corn oil
4 eggs
1 cup minced onion
1 cup shredded asadero or ranchero cheese (optional)
2 tablespoons minced seeded jalapeño chiles (optional)
2 tablespoons minced mixed bell pepper

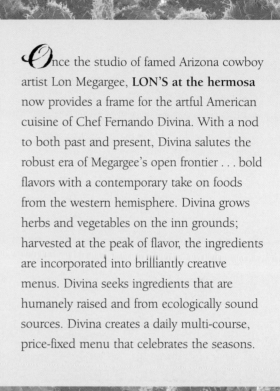

*O*nce the studio of famed Arizona cowboy artist Lon Megargee, **LON'S at the hermosa** now provides a frame for the artful American cuisine of Chef Fernando Divina. With a nod to both past and present, Divina salutes the robust era of Megargee's open frontier . . . bold flavors with a contemporary take on foods from the western hemisphere. Divina grows herbs and vegetables on the inn grounds; harvested at the peak of flavor, the ingredients are incorporated into brilliantly creative menus. Divina seeks ingredients that are humanely raised and from ecologically sound sources. Divina creates a daily multi-course, price-fixed menu that celebrates the seasons.

*P*reheat the oven to 375 degrees. Coat a 9×13-inch baking pan with oil and line the bottom with baking parchment or lightly oil and flour the baking pan. Combine the whole wheat flour, yellow cornmeal, blue cornmeal, sugar, baking powder and salt in a bowl and mix well. Whisk the milk, corn oil and eggs in a bowl until blended. Stir the onion, cheese, jalapeño chiles and bell pepper into the egg mixture and fold into the cornmeal mixture; do not overmix.

Spoon the batter into the prepared pan and bake until a wooden pick inserted in the center comes out clean. Serve immediately. For **Acorn Corn Bread,** substitute 2 cups acorn flour for the whole wheat flour. For **Potato Corn Bread,** substitute 1 1/2 cups potato flour for the whole wheat flour.

Sportsman's Fine Wine and Spirits recommends: Corn bread like this screams for a great beer. Something big and clean like Anchor Steam.

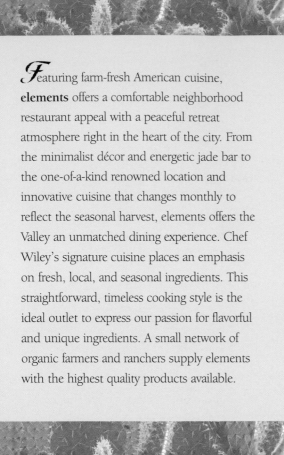

Featuring farm-fresh American cuisine, **elements** offers a comfortable neighborhood restaurant appeal with a peaceful retreat atmosphere right in the heart of the city. From the minimalist décor and energetic jade bar to the one-of-a-kind renowned location and innovative cuisine that changes monthly to reflect the seasonal harvest, elements offers the Valley an unmatched dining experience. Chef Wiley's signature cuisine places an emphasis on fresh, local, and seasonal ingredients. This straightforward, timeless cooking style is the ideal outlet to express our passion for flavorful and unique ingredients. A small network of organic farmers and ranchers supply elements with the highest quality products available.

Gingered Carrot and Toasted Millet Pot Stickers

Chef Charles Wiley of elements contributed this recipe.

Makes 2 dozen pot stickers

Soy Ginger Sauce
1/4 cup each soy sauce, mirin
  and water
2 garlic cloves, chopped
2 tablespoons rice
  wine vinegar
1 1/2 teaspoons brown sugar
1 teaspoon chopped
  fresh gingerroot
Cornstarch (optional)

Pot Stickers
1/4 cup millet
2 teaspoons minced fresh
  gingerroot

1 cup water
4 small carrots
2 tablespoons fat-free yogurt
2 tablespoons each roasted
  garlic and chopped
  fresh cilantro
Sea salt and pepper to taste
2 dozen round pot
  sticker wrappers
2 eggs, beaten
1 tablespoon cornstarch
2 teaspoons vegetable oil
1 cup vegetable stock
2 tablespoons chopped
  green onions

For the sauce, bring the first 7 ingredients to a boil in a saucepan; reduce the heat. Simmer for 5 minutes. Dissolve cornstarch in a small amount of cold water in a bowl and stir into the sauce. Cook until thickened, stirring constantly. Strain, discarding the solids, and cover to keep warm.

For the pot stickers, toast the millet in a dry saucepan over medium-high heat until it pops and turns golden brown. Stir in the gingerroot and cook briefly. Mix in the water and reduce the heat to low. Simmer, covered, until light and fluffy. Steam the carrots for 20 minutes. Let stand for 5 minutes to allow the moisture to evaporate. Mash the carrots in a bowl. Add the millet, yogurt, garlic, cilantro, salt and pepper and mash until combined. Spoon about 1 tablespoon of the millet mixture on each wrapper and brush the edges with the eggs. Fold over to enclose the filling and crimp the edges to seal. Dust a baking sheet with the cornstarch and arrange the pot stickers in a single layer on the prepared baking sheet to avoid sticking. Heat a nonstick skillet over medium-high heat and add the oil. Arrange the pot stickers crimped side up in batches in the hot skillet; do not crowd. Cook until brown and add some of the stock. Cook, covered, until the stock evaporates. To serve, ladle 2 tablespoons of the sauce in the center of 8 heated serving plates and arrange 3 pot stickers on each plate. Sprinkle with the green onions.

 Sportsman's Fine Wines and Spirits recommends: With all that spice and flavor, Gewürztraminer is the choice. My favorite is Trimbach Gewürztraminer from Alsace, France.

Cotija-Crusted Halibut with Green Chile Sauce

Chef Barbara Pool Fenzl of Les Gourmettes Cooking School contributed this recipe.

Serves 8

Green Chile Sauce

1¹/2 cups chicken stock

4 tomatillos, husked and chopped

1/4 cup chopped green onions

1 jalapeño chile, chopped

1 garlic clove, crushed

2 green Anaheim chiles, roasted, peeled, seeded and chopped

1/4 cup chopped fresh cilantro

1 tablespoon lime juice

Salt and pepper to taste

1 tablespoon heavy cream

Halibut

2 eggs

2 tablespoons water

2 cups panko

1 cup grated cotija cheese

2 teaspoons grated lemon zest

1/2 cup flour

8 (4- to 6-ounce) halibut fillets, skin removed

3 tablespoons olive oil

8 sprigs of cilantro

*F*or the sauce, bring the stock, tomatillos, green onions, jalapeño chile and garlic to a boil in a medium saucepan over medium-high heat; reduce the heat. Simmer for 15 to 20 minutes or until the liquid is reduced to 1 cup, stirring occasionally. Combine the hot stock mixture, Anaheim chiles, cilantro and lime juice in a blender or food processor and process until puréed. Return the mixture to the saucepan and season with salt and freshly ground pepper. Stir in the heavy cream. Keep warm over low heat.

For the halibut, whisk the eggs and water in a shallow dish. Mix the panko, cheese and lemon zest in a shallow dish. Spoon the flour into a shallow dish. Coat the flesh side of the fillets in the flour, shaking off the excess. Dip the flesh side in the eggs and coat the flesh side with the panko mixture and pat lightly. Preheat the oven to 400 degrees. Heat the olive oil in a nonstick baking pan over medium-high heat. Arrange the fillets crust side down in the oil. Sear for 4 minutes or until the crust is golden brown. Turn the fillets and roast for 3 to 5 minutes or until the centers are pearly white and opaque. To serve, spoon about 3 tablespoons of the sauce on each serving plate. Top each with 1 fillet and 1 sprig of cilantro.

 Sportsman's Fine Wines and Spirits recommends: I can always count on Pinot Grigio. One of the best is Bottega Vinaia Pinot Grigio, Trentino, Italy.

*T*he training I received as a member of The Junior League of Phoenix enabled me to reach long-term goals and play many different roles in the culinary world. The organizational skills I learned help me daily in operating **Les Gourmettes Cooking School**, which I founded in 1983. Leadership training was invaluable, as I served on three national boards and as president of the International Association of Culinary Professionals. Familiarity with communication techniques allowed me to host television shows, including my own PBS series, "Savor the Southwest," write two cookbooks, *Southwest the Beautiful Cookbook* and *Savor the Southwest*, as well as become a regular contributor to *Bon Appétit* and other magazines. But, most importantly, the Junior League taught me how important it is to give back to our community. My hat's off to the League for producing this delightful cookbook, which will provide funds to continue to improve the quality of life in the Valley of the Sun.

Southwestern Chicken Tart

Chef Jeff Blake of Arcadia Farms contributed this recipe.

Serves 6 to 8

Pastry
1 3/4 cups flour
1/2 teaspoon salt
1/2 cup (1 stick) unsalted
   butter, chilled and cut into
   1/2-inch cubes
1/4 cup shortening, chilled
3 to 5 tablespoons (or more)
   ice water

Chile Sauce
2 cups boiling water
4 ancho chiles, stemmed,
   seeded, veins removed
   and torn
1/2 cup chopped
   fresh cilantro
1/4 cup lime juice
1 jalapeño chile, stemmed,
   seeded, veins removed
   and coarsely chopped
3 garlic cloves
2 chipotle chiles in
   adobo sauce
1 cup sour cream
Salt and pepper to taste

Black Bean Layer
1 1/2 cups cooked or canned
   black beans, drained
   and rinsed
3/4 cup sour cream
1 teaspoon cumin
Salt and pepper to taste

Chicken Filling and
Assembly
1 red bell pepper, roasted,
   peeled, seeded and
   chopped
1 poblano chile, roasted,
   peeled, seeded and
   chopped
1 cup corn kernels, roasted
2 whole chicken breasts,
   poached, skinned, boned
   and shredded
1 cup (4 ounces) grated
   Parmesan cheese
1 cup (4 ounces) crumbled
   goat cheese
1 cup (4 ounces) shredded
   Swiss cheese

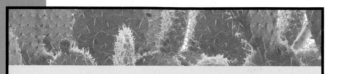

*A*rcadia Farms. . .farm-fresh organic
salads, delicious homemade desserts, fine
wines, and now, four artful locations:
luncheon is served at Phoenix Art Museum,
Desert Botanical Garden, Heard Museum, and
a charming circa 1953 Scottsdale cottage and
garden. Arcadia Farms was founded in 1990
by Carolyn Ellis, a graduate of Scottsdale
Culinary Institute and former banker. The
winner of numerous awards for her distinctive
cuisine, Ellis takes pride in a devoted staff of
professionals who help retain the loyalty of her
discerning restaurant and catering clientele.
Signature Arcadia Farms dishes include
Strawberry Chicken Salad, Roasted Vegetable
Tart, Raspberry Goat Cheese Salad, Warm
Grilled Salmon Salad, Key Lime Tart, Lemon
Cookies, and Chocolate Raspberry Cake.

*F*or the pastry, mix the flour and salt in a bowl. Add the butter and shortening and mix with a pastry blender until crumbly. Add the ice water and knead until the dough adheres without being too moist or sticky. Squeeze a small amount of the dough together, and if it is crumbly, add more ice water 1 tablespoon at a time. Wrap the dough in plastic wrap and chill for 30 minutes. You may prepare up to 1 day in advance and store, covered, in the refrigerator.

Roll the dough into a 14-inch round on a lightly floured surface using a floured rolling pin. Fit the round into a 10-inch fluted tart pan with a removable bottom. Trim the edge, leaving a 1/2-inch overhang. Fold the overhang inward and press against the side to reinforce the edge. Lightly prick the pastry with a fork and chill for 30 minutes.

Preheat the oven to 350 degrees. Line the chilled tart shell with foil or parchment paper and weight with pie weights or dried beans. Bake on the middle oven rack for 20 minutes or until the pastry is light brown along the edge. Discard the weights and foil and bake for 10 minutes longer or until the pastry is light brown. Let stand until cool.

For the sauce, combine the boiling water and ancho chiles in a heatproof bowl. Let stand for 30 minutes or until the chiles are rehydrated. Drain, reserving the liquid. Combine the cilantro, lime juice, jalapeño chile, garlic and chipotle chiles in a blender or food processor and process until puréed. Add the rehydrated ancho chiles and sour cream and process until smooth, adding the reserved liquid 1 tablespoon at a time for a thinner consistency. Season with salt and pepper.

For the black bean layer, process the beans, sour cream and cumin in a blender until puréed. Season with salt and pepper.

For the filling, preheat the oven to 350 degrees. Combine the sauce with the roasted bell pepper, poblano chile, corn and chicken in a bowl and mix well. You may prepare the filling up to 1 day in advance and store, covered, in the refrigerator. Sprinkle the Parmesan cheese over the bottom of the baked tart shell. Spread or pipe the bean mixture over the cheese. Layer with the filling, goat cheese and Swiss cheese. Bake for 15 to 25 minutes or until brown and bubbly and serve immediately.

 Sportsman's Fine Wines and Spirits recommends: For a spicy chile-laden entrée like this, a domestic Riesling would work well. One of my old standbys is Trefethin Dry Riesling, Napa Valley.

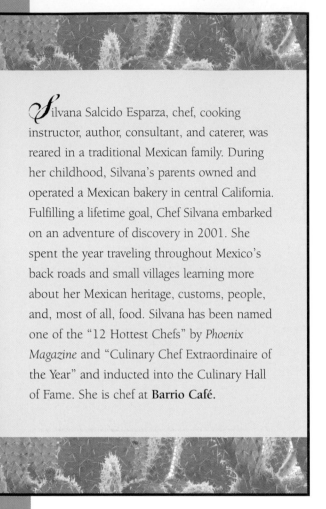

*S*ilvana Salcido Esparza, chef, cooking instructor, author, consultant, and caterer, was reared in a traditional Mexican family. During her childhood, Silvana's parents owned and operated a Mexican bakery in central California. Fulfilling a lifetime goal, Chef Silvana embarked on an adventure of discovery in 2001. She spent the year traveling throughout Mexico's back roads and small villages learning more about her Mexican heritage, customs, people, and, most of all, food. Silvana has been named one of the "12 Hottest Chefs" by *Phoenix Magazine* and "Culinary Chef Extraordinaire of the Year" and inducted into the Culinary Hall of Fame. She is chef at **Barrio Café.**

Cochinita Pibil (Mayan-Style Pit Pork with Sour Orange)

Chef Silvana Salcido Esparza of Barrio Café contributed this recipe.

Serves 8 to 10

4 ounces anchiote recado paste
Juice of 1 sour orange
1/4 teaspoon white wine vinegar
2 garlic cloves, minced
1/16 teaspoon Mexican oregano
2 large banana leaves
3 pounds pork roast or pork butt, trimmed
Salt and pepper to taste
2 cups water
Pickled red onions
Corn tortillas, warm
Yucatán-style salsa

*P*reheat the oven to 375 degrees. Combine the anchiote paste, orange juice, vinegar, garlic and oregano in a bowl and mix well. Trim the center core from the banana leaves and rinse with hot tap water until the leaves become soft and pliable; pat dry. Spread the leaves on a hard surface.

Place the roast in a bowl and sprinkle generously with salt and pepper and coat with the anchiote paste mixture. Arrange the roast on the banana leaves and wrap to enclose the surface completely.

Arrange the roast on a rack in a roasting pan. Add the water to the pan and tent with foil. Bake for 20 minutes and reduce the oven temperature to 300 degrees. Bake for 8 hours longer. Slice and serve with pickled onions, warm tortillas and salsa. You may substitute an equal mixture of grapefruit juice and lemon juice for the sour orange juice.

 Sportsman's Fine Wines and Spirits recommends: This recipe deserves not to be overpowered by a big red wine. . .try something that will complement, either a soft Syrah like Clos Mimi's Petite Rousse, Paso Robles, or a dry rosé like Saisons des Vins Le Printemps from Mendicno.

Pan-Roasted Halibut
with Artichokes
and Goat Cheese Salad

*Chef Robert Graham of Bistro 24 at The Ritz-Carlton contributed
this recipe.*

Serves 1

1 (8-ounce) halibut fillet

Salt and pepper to taste

2 tablespoons canola oil

1/2 cup marinated artichoke
heart halves

7 fingerling potato slices,
blanched

1/4 cup julienned sun-dried
tomatoes

1/4 cup caperberries

1 tablespoon minced garlic

2 teaspoons minced shallot

1/2 cup white wine

1 cup heavy cream

1/4 cup (1/2-inch) cubes goat
cheese

2 cups trimmed baby
spinach

2 tablespoons unsalted
butter

1 teaspoon minced shallot

1 teaspoon minced fresh
thyme

Bistro 24 is a popular local spot for people
watching and spotting the "who's who" of
Phoenix. The architecture is accented by blacks
and whites and enhanced by contemporary
décor and large plants throughout. The classic
marble and colorful murals subtly enhance the
overall visual effect. Ideal for the classic power
lunch, birthdays, romantic evenings, and private
parties, the smart and stylish restaurant offers
imaginative variations on classic bistro cuisine
in a comfortable indoor setting, or seasonal
outdoor dining on the patio. Sunday brunch is
outstanding, and patrons will find the central
location convenient with complimentary valet
parking. For reservations, call 602-952-2424
or visit our web site at www.ritzcarlton.com.

Preheat the oven to 350 degrees. Season the fillet with salt and pepper. Heat an ovenproof skillet
over medium heat and add the canola oil. Arrange the fillet presentation side down in the hot oil and
cook until brown; turn. Bake for about 6 minutes or until the fillet flakes easily.

Heat a sauté pan and add the artichokes, potato slices, sun-dried tomatoes and caperberries. Stir in the
garlic, 2 teaspoons shallot and wine and reduce. Add the heavy cream and cook until reduced by 1/2,
stirring constantly. Stir in the cheese and season with salt and pepper. Add the spinach and cook just
until the spinach is slightly wilted. Remove from the heat.

To serve, remove the fillet from the oven and add the butter, 1 teaspoon shallot and thyme to the hot
skillet and baste the fillet with the butter mixture. Spoon the spinach mixture into a round bistro bowl
and top with the fillet. Serve immediately.

Sportsman's Fine Wines and Spirits recommends: This dish would be a wonderful
match for a great Sauvignon Blanc. Try Spy Valley Sauvignon Blanc, Marlborough,
New Zealand.

ources

Arcadia Farms
7014 E. 1st Avenue
Scottsdale, AZ 85251
480-941-5665

The Arizona Kitchen at the Wigwam Resort & Golf Club
300 Wigwam Boulevard
Litchfield Park, AZ 85340
623-935-3811, ext. 1424

Barrio Café
2814 N. 16th Street
Phoenix, AZ 85006
602-636-0240

Bistro 24 at The Ritz-Carlton
2401 E. Camelback Road
Phoenix, AZ 85016
602-952-2424

Cowboy Ciao
7133 E. Stetson
Scottsdale, AZ 85251
480-946-3111

Durant's
2611 N. Central Avenue
Phoenix, AZ 85004
602-264-5967

Eddie V's Edgewater Grill
20715 N. Pima Road
Scottsdale, AZ 85255
480-538-8468

elements
5700 E. McDonald Drive
Paradise Valley, AZ 85253
480-607-2303

Franco's Italian Caffé
2501 E. Camelback Road
Phoenix, AZ 85016
602-381-1155

Les Gourmettes Cooking School
6610 N. Central Avenue
Phoenix, AZ 85012
602-240-6767

LON's at the hermosa
5532 N. Palo Cristi Road
Paradise Valley, AZ 85253
602-955-7878

Mancuso's
6166 N. Scottsdale Road
Scottsdale, AZ 85253
480-948-9988

Roaring Fork
4800 N. Scottsdale Road
Scottsdale, AZ 85251
480-947-0795

Zinc Bistro
15034 N. Scottsdale Road
Scottsdale, AZ 85255
480-603-0922

Recipe Contributors and Testers

A special thank-you to those who generously submitted their favorite recipes and graciously opened up their kitchens for testing. This cookbook would not have the tasteful collection it does without your input.

Caroline Aeed	Victoria Erickson	Jerry Lane	Brian Rugg
Chaunci Aeed	Theresa Esparza	Stephanie Larriva	Karen Rugg
Dana Alexander	Katherine Fore	Scott Larson	Richard Rugg
Sarah Anderson	Julie Foster	Stacey Larson	Suzi Rugg
Lynn Ault	Leah Furneaux	Pam Lowe	Renee Sacco
Ron Ault	Stefani Gambucci	Laura Mackey	Kim Sayre
Becky Babson	Melissa Gaspard	Sandy Mann	Kris Scardello
Glen Bachmann	Rob Gaspard	Christine Martin	Gena Seivert
Pamela Bachmann	Jennifer Geiger	Melissa Martin	Paul Seivert
Barbara Bauer	Marilyn Giles	Michele Martin	Kelly Smith
Priscilla Bilas	Courtney Gilstrap	Marjane McDougall	Monica Smith
Cathy Boyd	Mike Goldwater	Karin McFetters	Fae Sowders
Judy Brengi	Alicia Gonzalez	Heather McKinney	Carolyn Chapin Strandberg
Susan Brown	Cindy Good	Kim McQuaid	Fife Symington, III
Claudia Bullmore	Betsy Gorges	Stacey Meyer	Fife Symington, IV
Marie Burnett	Jacki Grainger	Kellie Moore	Marcella Billups Symington
June Camp	Ross Grainger	Mimi Moore	Faye Tait
Julie Campbell	Renee Grieve	Tim Moore	Donna Tardy
Patty Coleman	Leslie Guiley	Darcy Neill	Joan Tate
Ashley Crews	Alison Haueter	Kate Nelson	Erica TeKampe
Jan Crews	Carol Haueter	Jennifer Niccoli	Terri TeKampe
Jim Crews	Alice Henderson	Valerie Nikolaus	Stephanie Trahan
Kiley Crews	Catherine Herman	Christy Orders	Karen Treon
Ann Cross	Karen Jackowski	Susi Osborn	Andrea Tyler-Evans
Lynelle Crowell	Lucy Jackson	Monica Osselaer	Keri Van Fleet
Pamela Cullison	Susan Davenport Johnson	Rick Osselaer	Bob Villia
Allison Davis	Wendy Johnson	Bernice Pannuzzo	Chris Villia
Danielle Davis	Susan Jones	Nancy Pattyn	Karen Vivian
Nick Davis	Carol Kaslow	Lee Pistorius	Suzie Weathermon
Jane Dean	Yvette Katsenes	Susan Pistorius	Tina Wesoloskie
Barbara DeVoe	Brian Kevitt	Megan Pond	Wendy Wildt
Michelle DiMuro	Kristy Kevitt	Linda Powers	Jennifer Williams
Lyda DiTommaso-Espinosa	Gary Kiesler	Melanie Pullins	Janet Wilson
Tishin DonKersley	Jenny Kiesler	Tandy Richardson	Julie Wilson
Rosemary Duffey	Jill Kipnes	Chris Robbins	Kathy Wise
Karen Eiserloh	Randi Klingenberg	Holly Robbins	Ann Worthington
Paul Eiserloh	Annette Kracht	Jean Robbins	Jennifer Yeager
Pat Elder	Chris Kracht	Kiffie Robbins	Julie Yedlicka
Randy Elder	Jenny Lane	Elizabeth Ross	Ronelle Yee

$\mathcal{I}$ndex

Index

$\mathcal{I}$ndex

Index

JUNIOR LEAGUE OF PHOENIX
Women building better communities

The Junior League of Phoenix, Inc.

Cookbook Committee

P.O. Box 10223

Phoenix, Arizona 85064-0223

602-230-9573

www.jlp.org

Pomegranates & Prickly Pears

flavorful entertaining
from The Junior League of Phoenix

Name _____

Address _____

City _____ State _____ Zip _____

Telephone _____

Your Order	Quantity	Total
Pomegranates & Prickly Pears at $28.95 per book		$
Postage and handling at $6.00 per book		$
	Total	$

Method of Payment: [   ] MasterCard   [   ] American Express   [   ] Visa
[   ] Check(s) payable to The Junior League of Phoenix

Account Number _____   Expiration Date _____

Signature _____

Photocopies will be accepted.